GUY SPACES

GUY SPACES

A GUIDE TO DEFINING A MAN'S PERSONAL SPACE

Wayne Kalyn

CREATIVE HOMEOWNER®, Upper Saddle River, New Jersey

GUY SPACES

SENIOR EDITOR	Kathie Robitz
PHOTO EDITOR	Stan Sudol
PHOTO COORDINATOR	Robyn Poplasky
JUNIOR EDITOR	Jennifer Calvert
EDITORIAL ASSISTANT	Nora Grace
INDEXER	Sandi Schroeder
DIGITAL IMAGING SPECIALIST	Frank Dyer
DESIGN AND LAYOUT	David Geer
FRONT COVER PHOTOGRAPHY	(top, bottom right & left) Roger Wade; (center right) Stan Sudol
BACK COVER PHOTOGRAPHY	(top right) Roger Wade; (bottom right) Tria Giovan; (left) courtesy of Viking

CREATIVE HOMEOWNER

VICE PRESIDENT AND PUBLISHER	Timothy O. Bakke
PRODUCTION DIRECTOR	Kimberly H. Vivas
ART DIRECTOR	David Geer
MANAGING EDITOR	Fran J. Donegan

Current Printing (last digit)
10 9 8 7 6 5 4 3 2 1

Guy Spaces, First Edition
Library of Congress Control Number: 2007935570
ISBN-10: 1-58011-399-0
ISBN-13: 978-1-58011-399-1

CREATIVE HOMEOWNER®
A Division of Federal Marketing Corp.
24 Park Way
Upper Saddle River, NJ 07458
www.creativehomeowner.com

DEDICATION

To my son, Scott Richard—the joy of my life.

ACKNOWLEDGMENTS

Thank you to Neil Christensen of MultiSport Surfaces LLC in Hillsdale, New Jersey,
for his invaluable help and to the numerous homeowners who graciously allowed us
to photograph their property.

CONTENTS

INTRODUCTION

Looking for ideas for creating or remodeling rooms or areas in and around the house where guys love to spend their time? Need inspiration for converting an attic, basement, garage, or shed? How about cool ideas for a media or game room? No matter what your style or budget, you will find fresh takes on these areas and others, including bedrooms, baths, and gyms inside the house and sports courts, putting greens, and grilling spots outdoors. Here's your source for the latest information about everything from high-end personal spas to fully equipped auto workshops. *Guy Spaces* provides news about products and trends. Implement all or some of these ideas and you'll be the envy of your friends.

Right on cue. This open loft provides a fine spot for a billiards table. Good lighting enhances the game, and a small TV lets you keep tabs on your favorite sports events.

A PORTFOLIO OF IDEAS

This finished basement, below, has it all with a built-in refreshment center and a microwave oven for heating snacks.

Store your bike, opposite, properly over the winter or whenever you're not using it.

In Chapter 1, "Great Garages," you'll find easy solutions for makeovers that include the latest amenities. If you're interested in "Setting Up Shop," Chapter 2 has all the answers, including super workbench and storage options. Chapter 3, "Media and Game Rooms," connects you with the latest TV and sound technology. Watching the game at home is better than ever. Find out how to enhance the experience even more with media-wise ideas for furniture, lighting, and sound equipment. Complete the picture with a pool table and some arcade games.

Ready to flex some muscle? Chapter 4, "Game Courts and Home Gyms," offers a look at numerous custom-designed personal putting greens and game courts, including multisport courts and those for basketball, hockey, tennis, shuffleboard, tennis, bocce, and horseshoes.

After working up an appetite, you'll relish Chapter 5, "Grilling Spaces," which serves up a heap of ideas for everything from a small hibachi to a fully equipped outdoor kitchen.

Chapter 6, "Sheds," puts some light on your options for storage and more. Here's what you need to know, whether you build a shed from scratch or with help from a kit.

Finally, after work and play, Chapter 7, "Bedrooms, Bathrooms, and Storage," won't put you to sleep. You'll be amazed to see what you can do to create a one-of-a-kind masculine retreat that will make you forget the evening's traffic and get you ready to face it again in the morning.

CHAPTER 1

GREAT GARAGES

HUNTING FOR SPACE FOR A DELUXE WORKSHOP OR A GAME ROOM TO PLAY YOUR FAVORITE VIDEO GAMES? HOW ABOUT ROOM TO RESTORE A CLASSIC CAR OR FOR A PERSONAL GOLF STUDIO, COMPLETE WITH PUTTING GREEN AND VIDEO FACILITIES TO ANALYZE YOUR SWING? DON'T LOOK IN YOUR HOME FOR THAT EXTRA SQUARE FOOTAGE. LOOK OUTSIDE OF IT—TO YOUR GARAGE, AN OFTEN UNDERUSED SPACE. BUT AS MANY HOMEOWNERS ARE FINDING OUT, THE GARAGE IS FAR MORE THAN A SPACE TO PARK YOUR CAR OR AN ALL-PURPOSE STORAGE BIN FOR THE STUFF THAT DOESN'T FIT IN YOUR BASEMENT AND ATTIC. EVEN IF YOU DON'T WANT A SHOWPLACE, WHY NOT CONSIDER MAKING YOUR GARAGE CLEAN, SAFE, AND FUNCTIONAL? HERE ARE SOME IDEAS.

MULTIPURPOSE SPACE

THESE DAYS, GARAGES CAN BE REMODELED to serve many functions. In fact, garage renovations have become one of the fastest-growing areas of the remodeling business. It's no wonder—these conversions are easier and less expensive than putting up an addition. After all, a garage is fully enclosed and already comes with walls, a floor, and a ceiling. There's no need to spend major dollars breaking ground to expand your house.

What's more, no matter how grand your plan, remodeling your garage provides a major head start over new construction. The electric, plumbing, phone lines, and computer and TV cables are often accessible and can be easily upgraded or adapted to accommodate your design needs.

If you have a garage that is attached directly to your house, it offers a homeowner many remodeling possibilities. You can open a direct passage from your home to the new space, eliminating the need for exiting one structure to get to another—a bonus when the weather is hot or cold. An attached garage can conveniently increase your home's living space as a playroom, family room, or an extra bedroom.

A freestanding garage doesn't offer protection from the elements or the drive-in personal security of an attached garage. But it is ideal when greater separation from the main living space is desired—a home office, a studio to play your guitar, or a workshop with noisy power tools are just some of the options to consider.

A finished garage is a must-have for a serious car collector. Here, wall-to-wall built-in cabinetry stores automotive tools and media equipment.

Keep It Legal

BEFORE GETTING TOO INVOLVED with your plans, make sure your ideas for a garage conversion comply with local zoning regulations and state building codes. All building-code criteria must be met, such as structural integrity, ventilation, stairs, plumbing, and proper number and design of exits. In addition, you may have to provide alternative on-site parking when eliminating a parking space. Many municipalities don't permit additional street parking. Your new space can't interfere with the privacy of neighbors in adjoining properties, either. In some cases, the exterior elements of the garage may have to conform to the style of your house and neighborhood. If you fail to meet the required standards, you could be fined or forced to undo the work entirely. But don't panic yet, the project you have in mind may not even require a building permit—but find out to be sure.

A separate garage, below, may have to match the architecture of your house or the style of the neighborhood.

Add personality. Hawaiian hardwood paneling, right, is the perfect backdrop for a collection of surf boards.

ROOMS OF OPPORTUNITY

TRANSFORMING YOUR GARAGE doesn't mean you have to sacrifice your storage area. Many garages today have become multifunctional, allowing for cars, general storage, and a home office or workshop all in the same space. In addition to remodeling your current garage space, you could also consider building an addition above it. Raising the roof and adding a room for workspace above your existing garage can give you additional space without changing the floor plan.

It's hard to believe that this mess, above, was what existed before it was transformed into a spectacular wine garage, right. The air-conditioned room has a thermostat to maintain a cool and constant temperature of 60–65 deg. F, which is best for storing wine.

There are a number of possibilities for turning your garage into extra living space.

Home Office. If you telecommute and need privacy and quiet to get your work done, designing a home office in the out-of-the-way garage is a no-brainer. Just make sure to include enough electrical circuits to power all of your equipment as well as any add-on technology in the future.

Crafts Studio or Home Workshop. Perhaps you have a desire to try woodworking, refinish antique furniture, or work on some other hobby, but don't want to mess up rooms in your house or fill them with paint fumes and dust. An arts-and-crafts studio or home workshop, equipped with a quiet but powerful exhaust fan and a wall of storage bins, can solve both problems and provide the privacy to enable you to complete your projects.

Media Room. You don't need a fortune to create a highly entertaining media room for family and friends. It's easy to darken an already dim garage and to increase sound absorption with the right floor, wall, and ceiling materials. Cover windows if it's necessary. Are you ambitious? Include a snack bar or kitchenette, complete with a refrigerator, sink, and microwave oven, so you don't have to miss a minute of the movie.

One homeowner created this cool getaway where his son can study or listen to music. Folding glass doors overlook a small private deck.

Spa or Gym. After a hard day's work, wouldn't it be relaxing to soak in a hot tub or melt away the tension in a sauna? Or reinvigorate yourself with a spin on the treadmill or ellipical trainer? Look to your garage again. The concrete slab floor requires no additional structural reinforcement to handle the substantial weight of a hot tub, which can weigh more than 4,000 pounds when filled to capacity, or heavy gym machines. Saunas—which usually come as prefabricated packages, complete with walls, floor, and ceiling—are the perfect amenity for a windowless corner of the garage, and they can be tied into existing circuits.

Automotive Room. If working on cars is your passion, the garage is the perfect place for setting up shop. Your car, and most likely your tools, are already living in the garage, plus you have protection from the elements when working under the hood or on the car's interior. It's also easy to add extra lighting when you are trying to illuminate out-of-the-way nooks and crannies of an engine.

De-cluttering was key to reclaiming space in this old garage, which now boasts an organized and handsome custom look, right.

get started

« Make It Bright

Why stumble around in the dark? That's not safe or convenient. Make it easy to brighten a dark garage immediately by installing a light switch next to the door.

» TIP Add motion sensors to garage lights so they come on as soon as you open the door.

Easy Solutions During Makeovers

WHETHER YOU'RE CREATING a new room in your garage or just improving and organizing an existing space, there are some upgrades you should think about making. Start with lighting. One way to brighten your garage is by adding a couple of windows or skylights. Combining them with recessed lighting will be a big improvement, whether you're just storing or retrieving stuff from time to time or spending extended periods in the garage working on a hobby.

It's a good idea to add more electrical outlets. Install them on the wall approximately every 34 inches so you won't trip over extension cords while working on a project. Also, add a few outlets on the ceiling for extra convenience. In addition, heavy-duty power tools, such as a table saw, should have their own dedicated 220-volt line.

Another smart improvement would be to add insulation. Be sure to insulate the space between wood studs, whether you're adding walls or not. It will cut your energy bills and soundproof the space at the same time. There are numerous kinds of insulation, depending on the type of ceiling material. Fiberglass ceiling batts can be faced or unfaced and are typically precut to fit between rafters. They can be placed directly on top of the existing ceiling or on top of ceiling pan-

els. Cellulose insulation, made from recycled newspapers, can be blown in to fill the spaces between rafters.

To keep the garage comfortable, replace the garage door. You can lose as much as 30 percent of your home's heat through an old door. New models made of steel and composite materials have insulated cores containing polystyrene or other materials. They not only have a higher R-value (the capacity of a material to impede heat flow) than garage doors made of wood but also stand up well to the weather. New garage doors also come with energy-efficient double-pane glass.

State-of-the-art garage-door openers are very quiet, fast, and safe. Look for one that has a remote control with rolling security codes instead of a fixed code to prevent thieves from stealing it. Most new garage-door openers have electric eye-type sensors to reverse the door if a child or pet is underneath it. Adding an automatic garage-door closer at the same time makes sense. They're easy to install with an existing opener, and they can be programmed to close anywhere from two minutes to an hour after the door was opened.

New garage doors can help to insulate the space as well as improve the exterior appearance of your home. Those made of steel or composite materials are low-maintenance, too.

Your Comfort Zone

Good ventilation and cooling are two more things that help to make a finished or converted garage comfortable and livable. Increase air flow by installing windows, ceiling fans, and even a quiet but powerful exhaust fan with an adjustable gooseneck to displace high levels of heat and humidity as well as fumes from paints and chemicals. A wall-mounted air conditioner—or tying into your home's central air-conditioning systems—can help keep you cool in summer.

Heating. If you're turning the space into a year-round living area, baseboard heating or a new heating system incorporated into an existing gas or oil system will take care of your needs.

If you'll be using the space sporadically, portable ceramic space heaters can take the chill out of the air in a small- to medium-size space. Kerosene heaters are also useful. Easy to start, most have an electric heater and can really kick out the heat. The kerosene odor does bother some people, so make sure that the room is well ventilated. For large spaces, look to professionally installed gas heaters: most smaller units can heat an area up to 1,000 square feet, the size of a two-car garage.

In an automotive room, finished walls and floors provide a clean backdrop for pampering a collection of vintage cars, while cabinets store equipment.

More Amenities

TODAY'S REMODELED GARAGES have evolved into living spaces that are as comfortable and full of amenities as the rooms in the house. Nothing makes a room feel cozier than a toasty-warm fireplace. Some of today's gas or electric models also come with a heater. Tying into the home's gas lines, direct-vent fireplaces expel gases to the outside. Direct-vent fireplaces can heat the redesigned space in winter and will even work in the case of electrical failure.

A ventless gas fireplace is another option. Efficiency is this fireplace's first and middle name. All the heat produced by a ventless gas fireplace is retained within the space. Most ventless gas fireplaces are required to include an oxygen depletion sensor (ODS), a safety feature that warns if oxygen levels in the room are becoming low. These fireplaces work in the event of power outages.

This 21-cu.-ft. refrigerator has an upscale stainless-steel look. If you need more space for extra soft drinks, the freezer compartment converts into additional refrigerator storage.

If your garage isn't cooled by your home's central air conditioner, a portable model can do it. A flexible hose vents the hot exhaust to the outside, usually through a window kit that you attach to a windowsill.

Finally, check out some of the compact appliances on the market. If you want to design a cozy snack area for a media room or create a galley kitchen in your home office, there are scaled-down appliances that can easily fit into small areas—everything from 21-inch-wide stoves to 8.6-cubic-foot refrigerators and mini-dishwashers. Check out modular (and expensive) drawer-size models, too.

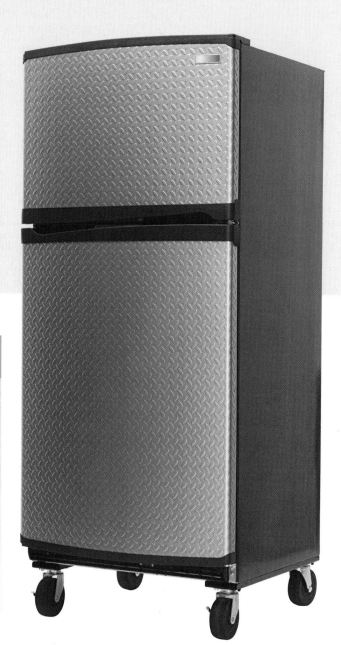

ONE MORE THING ...

Parking Guides

LASER PARKING GUIDES typically attach to the ceiling on or near the garage-door opener. When the garage door is opened the laser is activated and lights up a beam. Align the beam with a particular spot on your dashboard to park your car in the same place every time. Proximity sensors mount on the wall. You preset the distance between your bumper and the sensor, and the sensor will tell you when to stop every time you pull in and park.

STYLE THAT WILL FLOOR YOU

These days, you can have the same wide range of flooring choices for the garage as you do for the rest of your home. The function of the room dictates the type of floor you install. Expensive parquet flooring isn't practical in a home workshop, and thin vinyl mats wouldn't work well in a plush media room. Here are some of the most popular choices to consider:

Carpeting softens the hard concrete slab found in most garages and provides coziness and warmth to a home office or hobby room. In rooms where you want to confine sound, such as a media room, carpet is indispensable. Some come with an antimicrobial treatment that resists mold and mildew. Others are stain-resistant.

If you're planning to convert the garage into living space, a *hardwood* floor is a great idea. You'll find dozens of finishes and configurations—strip planks, parquet squares, self-stick squares, as well as prefinished options. Although it adds warmth and is easy underfoot, hardwood is expensive and must be maintained and refinished eventually. If hardwood is out of your budget, a laminate offers the look of natural wood, but it's resistant to moisture or dampness—and it's more affordable. You can't refinish it like wood, however, and you will have to replace it when it wears.

Available in sheets or tiles, *resilient vinyl* is easy to maintain and is comfortable underfoot. The tiles are easy to install or replace yourself if you have a level floor. Vinyl comes in an almost endless selection of colors and styles, including wood, tile, and faux stone. It is an excellent choice for high-activity rooms or areas that might be exposed to water.

Other options include *PVC floor mats.* These are easy to install and durable covering for stained or fissured concrete floors. You can butt the mats together for a virtually seamless look. This option provides a cushion if you will be on your feet for long lengths of time.

There's also *synthetic modular flooring squares.* Simply snap the polyvinyl squares together to form any number of handsome patterns. They are resistant to petroleum products and most household chemicals—and are easy to clean. Just hose off or mop the squares. Unlike stains and epoxy paints, there are no toxic fumes or wait time for it to dry.

Nonporous garage flooring that comes in sheets, below, or interlocking tiles, bottom, is chemical resistant and can withstand temperature extremes.

Concrete Ideas

ACID-STAINED CONCRETE can create a warm finish in multiple hues and colors. Unlike coatings that you can paint over and adhere to concrete, acid stain chemically reacts and soaks into it. With acid stain you can create the look of stone or leather, but you do have to apply a protective seal coat to prevent damage to the look.

You can also apply an epoxy coating to concrete. It forms a hard, durable surface and strong bond to a concrete surface and resists any chemicals that you might spill on it. Epoxy coating can be difficult to apply and takes several days to dry.

Latex is the least-expensive option. There are several types of acrylic paints designed for garage floors. Once you have applied the paint, you can usually walk on the floor in four hours and park on it after 72 hours.

A sealed concrete floor is practical and good looking. You can stain the concrete almost any color and you can also create numerous deorative effects, such as textures or inlays.

» TIP Before applying stain or coatings, test the concrete's moisture level by taping a 3 x 3-ft. piece of landscaping plastic to the floor and check for condensation on the underside after a few days. If moisture is present, don't apply a coating—it will eventually bubble up.

DECK THE WALLS

THESE DAYS IT IS EASY to cover garage walls with any number of man-made or natural materials that will enhance the look and livability of the room. After you add insulation and drywall, there is no limit to the style you can achieve in your new space.

Perhaps the first choice for many homeowners, *paint* is an inexpensive way to add color.

Brick or *stone veneer* will add a rustic look to your garage room, or it can function as an attractive fireproof backing for a wood-burning stove. Solid stone and brick are heavy and may require additional support. New cast-stone products, which imitate natural stone and brick, are thinner, weigh less, and are easy to install.

Paneling is no longer restricted to the knotty-pine planks of the 1950s rec room. Real-wood veneers or tongue-and-groove paneling come prefinished or ready for painting or staining.

Plywood known as *T1-11* is a composite plywood with either smooth, stucco, or wood-grain surfaces. It works great in a workshop space in a garage. Besides being hard to dent, it also offers optimum flexibility for hanging items on the wall.

A flexible wall system, top right, can be a do-it-yourself project or you can hire a professional installer to do it for you.

This brick wall, right, has a particularly traditional appeal to it, especially paired with the horizontal planks of blond pine paneling.

ONE MORE THING ...

WHEN INSTALLING DRYWALL in rooms that are damp, use the moisture-resistant type. It can be distinguished from traditional drywall by its green color.

Ceilings To Look Up To

The type of ceiling you choose depends mostly on how you'll use the new space. If your main use is storage, drywall will do. For use as a living space, you may want to install ceiling paneling. If the space will be used as a workshop or family room, consider noise-dampening acoustical tile.

Drywall is the least-expensive ceiling material to install and goes up relatively fast. It can be painted to match the decor. Although many design pros will tell you that the only color for a ceiling is white, it's also true that you can change a room's appearance for the better with a little color.

Ceiling paneling has recently become popular, thanks to some of the new installation methods that manufacturers have designed. With a snap-in-place system, the panels go up in an afternoon. Most ceiling paneling is covered with laminate, so it doesn't require any special care.

Acoustical tile goes up similarly to ceiling paneling and also does a great job of concealing a bad ceiling. Acoustical tile comes in many patterns and almost always in white. It is available in 12- and 24-inch squares. This type of ceiling is a smart choice for a media room where you want to contain the rich sound.

The vaulted ceiling and wood beams lift the look of this garage to new heights. Details, such as the clerestory windows, wood paneling, dentil molding, and the warm color of the stain, make this space as bright and appealing as any modern cabin.

Windows: Let in the Light

WHETHER YOU'RE CONVERTING A GARAGE to living space or just want to bring more light into a dimly lit garage, you'll need to select from a range of window types. Here are several of the most common styles:

• **Single and Double-Hung.** The difference between a single- and double-hung window is the ability of the upper sash to move. On a single-hung window, it's fixed; with a double-hung, it can be raised or lowered. The lower sash on both types is movable. When shopping for either window, look for the tilting-sash variety, which tilt out for easy cleaning.

• **Casement.** A casement window is one in which the sash is hinged on the side to allow it to pivot in and out like a door. Casement windows provide significantly better ventilation than sliding windows of equal size.

• **Awning.** Awning windows are hinged at the top and swing open at the bottom. Just like casement windows, awning windows provide greater ventilation than sliding windows because practically the entire window area can be opened. Awning windows can be installed so the sash opens outward (such as in a garage or workshop) or inward in the case of a basement window.

• **Sliding.** Sliding windows are inexpensive because there are fewer moving parts than in the other types of windows mentioned above. On most sliding windows, one half of the window is fixed and the other half slides back and forth in a track.

• **Skylights.** Skylights are a great way to get a lot of light into your garage. Some slimmer skylights are designed to fit between ceiling joists. Otherwise, the best time to install a skylight is when you're replacing the roof—after the old shingling is torn off and before the new shingles are put down.

• **Tubular Skylights.** Tubular skylights capture sunlight on the roof and redirect it down through a highly reflective tube and into your room. Their graceful circular shape can be more handsome than a traditional skylight and will flood the space with sunlight.

• **Glass or Acrylic Blocks.** For light, privacy, and energy efficiency, block windows of glass or lightweight acrylic make sense in an exterior wall. They let in more natural light, making interior spaces seem more spacious. They also protect your privacy by partially obscuring the view. Glass-block windows are also energy efficient, cutting your heating bill.

Glazing Options

The types and number of panes in a window will affect its insulating properties.

- **Single Pane.** This is the least energy-efficient window. One option you might consider is upgrading to a double- or triple-pane window with a low-E coating applied to it. This coating filters out ultraviolet rays to protect furnishings while also helping to insulate the space in winter and summer.

- **Double Pane.** A double-pane window has two panes of glass separated by an air space. When sealed properly, this air space provides insulation from both summer heat and winter cold. To further increase the insulating properties of the window, some manufacturers inject a safe, colorless gas (such as argon) into this space.

- **Triple Pane.** The ultimate in insulated windows is the triple pane. Three panes of glass offer two separate insulating spaces. Here again, these spaces can be filled with argon or another gas to increase the insulating properties of the window. Both double- and triple-pane windows will keep your living space quieter, significantly reducing noise transmission.

Windows installed high on the walls, opposite left, admit light and air without sacrificing privacy.

Garage-door windows, opposite right, come in a number of styles, some with snap-in grilles or etching.

A converted garage, below, has French doors and casement windows overlooking the garden.

STORAGE SOLUTIONS

WHETHER YOU'RE PLANNING additional space, giving your garage an organizational face-lift—or doing both—there are any number of solutions for keeping stuff in one place and at your fingertips.

In an unfinished garage, you can make good use of the exposed studs and slats by hanging things on nails or hooks attached to the fronts or sides of the studs themselves or from the support ledge between the studs. Peg-Board, another option, is nothing new to home garages, but it is one of the most versatile types of organizers you can use. What is new is the innovative shelves, hooks, bins, and containers that fit into it these days. While basic Peg-Board is a little flimsy, you can strengthen it by adding more support when you mount it. New types of Peg-Board made from metal and plastic are stronger than the old kind.

One standard solution is devoting an entire wall—perhaps a back wall—to a series of closets that can house everything from out-of-season clothes to sporting equipment. Think vertically as well, using every inch of space when planning shelving. When outfitted with wood-louver doors that allow air to circulate, closets look good, too. When buying a shelving system, look for one that is adjustable so that you can reconfigure the shelves as your needs change.

Freestanding metal or wooden shelving units work well with a bin and basket system and can be easily arranged according to your needs. Additional shelves, as well as sliding drawers and storage baskets, hook on the side of the unit and can be purchased individually. The downside is the unit's lack of mobility.

A system of freestanding and wall-mounted cabinets, below left, provides uniform storage.

Some things can hang from hooks that attach to the the wall panels, below right.

ONE MORE THING ...

LEAVE ANY PEG-BOARD (or other wall paneling) in the room where it will be installed for 24 hours to allow the panels to adjust to the room's moisture level. This will prevent the board from warping.

Wall-mounted shelving is great for maximizing wall space and getting things off the floor. One of the key advantages of these systems is their flexibility: the shelves are fully adjustable. Choose wire shelving over wood so you can see the shelf contents and to allow for better circulation to prevent mold and mildew.

One of the more popular ways to both add storage to your garage and enhance its looks is to install a grooved wall-panel system. Available in five colors, the panels are made of PVC and screwed to the walls. Grooves in the panels accept a variety of accessories (even cabinets) ranging from wire shelving and baskets to plastic bins and hooks.

Track-style storage, consisting of rails, cabinets, and accessories, can be integrated to create a coordinated, finished look. The rails are attached to wall studs and accept a wide variety of specialty holders that support everything from a wheelbarrow and bikes to power tools and sports equipment.

The ceiling is one of the most underutilized storage spaces in a garage. Make use of it by installing a ceiling-mounted shelving system that allows you to store items up and out of the way. The shelving is available up to 8 feet wide and can be adjusted from 17 to 30 inches from the ceiling as your storage needs change.

Finally, closed-door cabinetry systems are the ultimate in organization. They give your garage a clean, professional look and offer the benefit of lockable storage. In addition, cabinets offer built-in organization in the form of shelving and drawers. Freestanding units can be outfitted with wheels for easy mobility and cleanups. Cabinets are available in all types of materials: laminate, anodized aluminum, and wood.

Freestanding units on legs let you clean the floor underneath the cabinets. For safety, some of these units can be locked.

Rules for Shelves

1. Shelves should be deep enough to safely store items, yet not so deep that items will get hidden behind each other.

2. Shelves should always be adjustable to maximize the use of space. It's better to have more shelves and space them closer together than to stack objects too high on a single shelf.

3. Store frequently used items on shelves at waist height, where they're easier to access; store items used less frequently on higher or lower shelves.

4. Keep newer backup replacement items behind older items on the shelf, similar to the way items are displayed on a grocery store shelf. That way, you use the older things first.

There are all kinds of shelving systems, including wall-mounted designs and freestanding units that you can combine to suit your garage size and storage needs. Shelves made of plastic, including open-wire units, are the most practical because they won't warp and they are easy to wipe clean. To make the most of space, store anything that gets little use on a high shelf.

GARAGE DOOR STYLES

GARAGE DOORS COME IN COUNTLESS STYLES these days to fit the architecture and feel of your home. There are four popular types today. Spanish-Style has wood timbers that add decorative black-iron hardware to create a look that would work well in a Spanish hacienda, a Mediterranean villa, or a contemporary Santa Fe-style home. Mission (or Craftsman) style features short or long panels and comes with a variety of window and grille options to create a look that fits in with a mission-style or Craftsman home. The windows can be rectangular or arched.

Sleek, modern lines combined with high-tech materials such as anodized aluminum are the perfect complement to contemporary or modern homes. But if your tastes lean more traditional, carriage style is for you. Reminiscent of the doors that adorned carriage houses of yesteryear, carriage-style doors offer a classic look. These days traditional carriage-style doors come with the strength and durability of steel and are virtually maintenance free.

ONE MORE THING ...

Common Garage Sizes

ONE-CAR GARAGE	12 x 24 ft.
TWO-CAR GARAGE	24 x 24 ft.
THREE-CAR GARAGE	36 x 24 ft.
FOUR-CAR GARAGE	48 x 24 ft.

Carriage-style garage doors, above, enhance the overall look of the property.

The frames around the garage doors, below, blend well with the slope of the roofline.

CHAPTER 2

SETTING UP SHOP

WORKSHOPS ARE GREAT PLACES TO EXPLORE A CREATIVE PASSION, WHETHER THAT IS WOODWORKING, RESTORING A CLASSIC CAR, BUILDING A SAILBOAT OR FURNITURE, OR DOING SOME ALL-PURPOSE CARPENTRY. AWAY FROM THE BUZZ OF HOUSEHOLD ACTIVITY, YOU CAN HEAR YOURSELF THINK. AND WHEN YOU'RE READY TO BUILD, DEPENDING ON THE DESIGN OF YOUR HOME—AND THE SCALE OF THE PROJECTS—THE BASEMENT, ATTIC, GARAGE, OR AN ENCLOSED PORCH ARE GOOD LOCATIONS FOR SETTING UP SHOP.

ATTICS ALREADY HAVE LIGHTING AND ELECTRICAL SERVICE AND ARE USUALLY INSULATED. BECAUSE ACCESS IS TYPICALLY UP A NARROW STAIRWAY, WHICH MAKES MOVING LARGE EQUIPMENT AND MATERIALS DIFFICULT, YOU MAY BE LIMITED TO KEEPING HAND TOOLS OR SMALLER MODELS OF POWER TOOLS IN AN ATTIC SHOP. FORTUNATELY, BENCH-TOP MODELS OF MOST WOODWORKING MACHINES ARE READILY AVAILABLE.

What about the basement? With existing electrical service, lighting, and often a sink and running water, a basement is an ideal place for a home shop. Another advantage of a basement shop is built-in temperature control. It's typically cool even on hot summer days and, because the heated house stands above it, a basement is comfortable on all but the coldest days of winter.

What if you've already finished the attic or the basement for extra living space? Take a look at your garage. The average two-car garage is another ideal place for a workshop because it has a large entry door that makes it easy to move lumber and bulky materials in and out with ease. The floor—typically a concrete slab—is level and weatherproof. In addition, your garage may already be outfitted with 220-volt electricity, which is needed to run large machines.

Still looking for space? An attached, enclosed porch may offer enough room to set up a small workshop. Because the porch is attached to the house, one wall already exists and the other walls can be fitted between the porch's roof support. If it isn't already there, electrical service is readily accessible, too.

Look to a double garage to create a fully equipped workshop. This one, below, includes a portable work island, overhead light, and plenty of work space.

A woodworking shop should include storage above and below the workbench, overhead and task lighting, and a specialized workstation for cutting or routing wood, opposite.

WITH A PLAN IN MIND

WORK OUT A DESIGN for your shop on paper before purchasing any large equipment in order to make sure there's enough space for it. You'll also find that a thoughtfully planned design will make the best use of the space, whatever its size. Your objective should be to create a shop that is comfortable and efficient.

For most workshops, a work triangle is best, with the three main focuses of your hobby or craft needs located at the three corners. In a shop geared toward woodworking, for example, storage for wood and lumber, along with large power tools such as a table saw and jointer, can be positioned in one corner of the triangle. Next, locate the workbench in the second corner, which is usually in the center of the room. This is where you could use hand tools or small power tools such as a hand drill or router. The finishing station can then be located in the third corner, where fine, detailed work could take place.

The triangle is just a conceptual guideline, and the actual goal is efficiency. Ultimately, you'll have to create a layout that suits you as a comfortable and convenient place to work.

WORKSHOP UPGRADES

A slat-wall storage system holds cabinets of all sizes and heights.

WHETHER YOU'RE JUST CREATING A WORKSHOP for your new hobby, or thinking about sprucing up an old space, you should review a few basics. Do you have, or have you planned, adequate electrical service for your equipment? What needs to be done about heating or cooling the space? How will you finish the walls and floors? Make sure your plans are covering all bases now, not after you've completed the project. You don't want to have to rip out a wall to add more electrical receptacles.

Electrical

LARGE WORKSHOP EQUIPMENT such as table saws or air compressors should be powered via dedicated circuits. In addition, a ground-fault circuit interrupter (GFCI) receptacle will shut down the power in the circuit immediately in case of a short. This will reduce the possibility of electric shock.

It's hard to have too many electrical receptacles in a workshop. A good rule of thumb is to install them around the entire room, spacing them 36 inches apart. Also consider what point on the wall you want to locate the receptacles in order to provide the most convenient access to the work surfaces and your equipment.

A power strip is an easy way to gain more outlets in an existing shop without having to put holes in the walls and run wire. Most of them include a small circuit breaker so that you won't accidentally overload the capacity of the power strip's wiring.

Always be sure to include storage above the workbench to enable easy access to tools. Using an adjustable wall system allows similar tools to be stored together so the right one can be found quickly or the space rearranged as more tools are added.

Walls and Floors

If you don't mind a bit of sanding and painting, it's smart to finish the walls with wallboard, which is readily available and inexpensive. While its heavy weight makes it a chore to install on high walls and ceilings, its density helps to reduce the amount of machine noise that escapes from the shop. Drywall tends to reflect high-frequency noise, but workshop shelves and cabinets help to dampen it. Paint it a light color to keep the space bright.

Another way to go is with relatively lightweight and inexpensive wood paneling. However, in some places you have to install wood paneling over a fire-resistant backing of wallboard, so find out from the building department in your town beforehand. Sheets typically measure 4 x 8 feet and are ¼ to ¾ inch thick and they are easy to cut and trim. Choose a light-color finish to help bounce and diffuse workshop lighting.

If your shop has a concrete floor, two coats of concrete paint will hide ugly stains. Use a light color, which is reflective and will help to make the space brighter. Concrete floors are porous, so first apply a masonry sealer to prevent water seepage. A sealant will also protect the floor against oil stains, tire tracks, and other types of grime. To prevent slipping accidents from spilled liquids or oil, mix clean sand into the paint to provide grit and traction.

If you're building a new shop, a wood floor is cozy and easy on the feet. An alternative for the budget minded is a laminate floor, which is easy to install, too. If you can spend a little more, consider adding a radiant-heating system under the floor to keep the space even warmer. Using an interlocking floor-tile system is another option that offers layout flexibility and protection for your knees. If you move equipment around—or if you move to a new shop—you can reconfigure the tiles.

What else can you do? Cover your shop's cold, hard floor with rubber floor mats—also called antifatigue mats. In work areas and in front of machines, these mats can make standing for long periods of time a lot more comfortable and easier on your knees and feet.

This handsome wall of stainless-steel cabinets, left, can hold everything from large power tools to smaller items, such as hammers and screw drivers.

Adding a special magnetic bar to a wall-slat system keeps a full complement of hand tools always within easy reach, opposite.

get started

« Make It Work

If you need traction, choose a commercial-grade flooring with a tread pattern. If your shop activities will generate a lot of debris or spills, a ribbed pattern will make cleaning up easier.

» **TIP** Coin-pattern industrial flooring is a good choice when you need a tough floor that looks good, too.

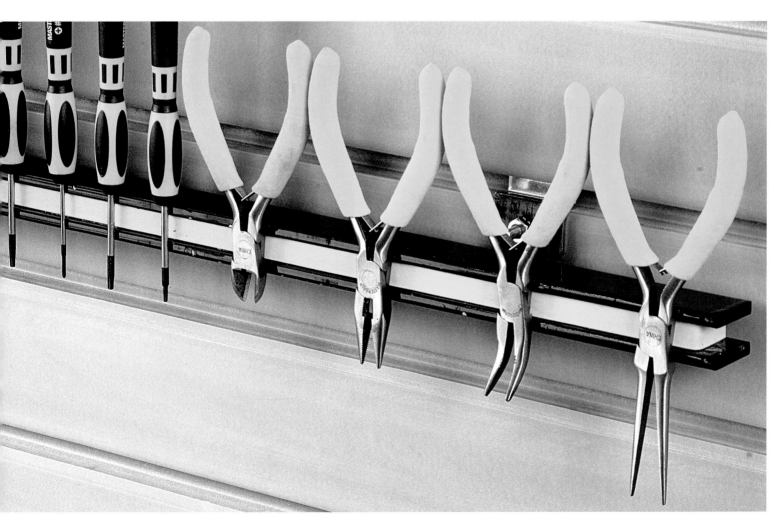

CHAPTER 2: SETTING UP SHOP

Doors

IF YOUR WORKSHOP is in a garage, you have more than enough room to move large machines in and out of the space. Double doors are a wise choice in other structures. You can use one door for everyday comings and goings, and use both doors when you have to move in a large piece of lumber or move out the sailboat you just built. Wherever possible use solid doors rather than hollow-core units to muffle loud noise.

Insulation. Install weather stripping on doors for dust and noise control, not to mention extra insulation in the walls, floors, and ceiling to keep noises from disturbing the rest of the house—or the neighbors in case the workshop is located in a detached garage.

Use insulated doors between the shop and main house to cut down on noise, below.

A handsome French door allows plenty of natural light into this workshop, right.

Heating and Cooling

Don't forget to consider heating and cooling needs. If you have a zone-controlled heating and cooling system, you could extend it to a shop located in a space that is attached to your house. Otherwise, because of their low cost and flexibility of use, portable heaters are the single most attractive solution for a small shop. Propane and kerosene heaters are easy to start and cheap to run, providing a steady stream of heat. Electric ceramic heaters are a good means of heating small workspaces rapidly. They can be easily moved around, depending on where you're working in the shop. Heaters can also be installed in the toe-kick area if you'll have built-in cabinets—like the base cabinets in your kitchen—in the shop.

To keep a shop cool in the hotter months, you can use fans, a wall- or window-mounted air conditioner, or a portable air conditioner that vents hot exhaust through a window to the outside. Using sun-blocking curtains or insulated blinds on windows, skylights, and doors can help to reduce heat from the sun, as well as block drafts from getting into the workshop.

Dehumidifiers

Humidity in a workshop can rust tools and be absorbed by lumber and other materials. Dehumidifiers are an easy way to remove humidity from the air. It can be challenging to purchase the right-size machine to do the job. Units are rated by how many pints of water per hour—usually 25, 40, or 50—they can remove from the air. To determine your needs, multiply the length and width of your room to figure out square feet. A 25-pint machine can service most basements of 500 to 2,000 square feet that are moderately damp or very damp. You'll probably need a 40- or 50-pint machine for 2,500 square feet or more.

To save energy, look for automatic models that shut off once a preset level of humidity is reached.

For top efficiency, close the doors and windows to make sure fresh, humid air doesn't flow into the basement while your dehumidifier is running. In warm climates, consider dehumidifying a basement with a window- or wall-mounted air-conditioner instead of a dehumidifier, which adds heat to an already warm space. For your convenience, buy a machine that allows you to drain the water through a hose or tube directly into a floor drain or sump pump.

Dust and Debris Collection. Woodworking shops produce a lot of dust. Install a dust collection system to keep it under control. Without one, dust will find its way into forced-air heating and cooling systems and settle throughout the house. Connect vacuum hoses to every power tool. To clean up dust and other debris from the workshop floor and walls, use a powerful wet-dry vacuum. New models are quieter than previous models and are equipped with upgraded filters that capture particles as small as 0.3 microns.

State-of-the-art automated vacuums sweep workshop floor surfaces as you work. The high-speed, counter-rotating brushes and extra-large dust bin pick up and store woodchips, nuts, bolts, dirt, and other heavy duty debris until you're ready to empty them into the trash.

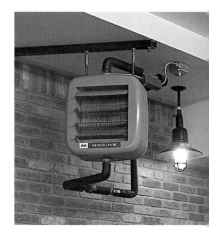

A heavy-duty overhead fan, above, can vent fumes and sawdust from the workspace.

Durable rubber mats or interlocking tiles, below, catch messes and spills and are easy to clean, as well as comfortable.

WORKBENCHES

A WORKBENCH is an essential fixture for any job site or workshop. Portable or permanent, equipped with drawers, vises, or a drafting-table tilt top, a bench not only helps work go faster and more accurately, it also keeps you safe. Workbenches come in all shapes in sizes. Small, foldable ones can travel from job to job, while heavy, furniture-like pieces with drawers and cabinets become a permanent fixture in the workshop. Most permanent benches have standard tops set near counter height (36 inches). But adjustable benches are handy if you want to tailor them to your own height and the tools with which you're working. Here is a quick rundown of the three most common types of workbenches.

Portable Workbench. This type of bench enables the user to move it wherever it is needed in the workshop. Many models can be adjusted to varying heights and have detachable casters. Some come with the option of a leveling mechanism or feet that allow you to set your tools straight or work on uneven surfaces, such as your driveway, if you need to roll the workbench outdoors to tackle a specific job. Portable workbenches can hold large and small tools, and some models are designed to serve as a shop bench, router station, or clamping station.

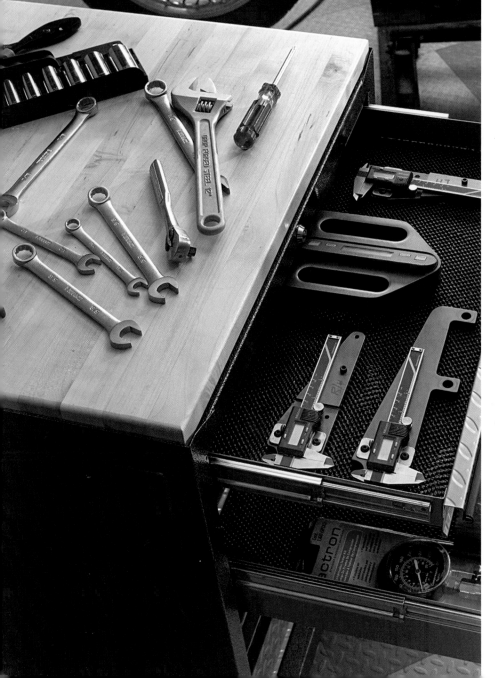

Workbenches with rubber-lined drawers, left, can keep tools from becoming a jumble.

Portable workbenches and tool caddies, below, can be rolled wherever you might need them in the shop.

Stationary Workbench. A stationary workbench, weighing up to a couple of hundred pounds, is a sturdier alternative to portable benches that are not recommended for loads that are more than a couple of hundred pounds. It should measure at least 2 x 5 feet and can cost anywhere from $100 to $1,000 or more, depending on its size and construction. The better ones include drawers and cabinets, so tools and materials are always at hand. It can go in the middle of the shop so you can walk around it for woodworking or up against a wall for general storage and projects.

Folding Workbench. A folding workbench is ideal when workshop space is at a premium. This type of workbench offers easy storage and a stable broad base. Many models come with a tabletop clamping device to secure work to the table.

When you're deciding where to put a workbench, leave enough clearance around machines and cabinets so you will have adequate space in which to work. If your shop is small or crowded, placing a workbench along the wall conserves valuable floor space, freeing up the room for working on large projects.

Sawhorses. These handy devices can provide the base for a decent portable work surface. Set them outside on a beautiful day, place a piece of sturdy plywood or an old hollow-core door on top, and you have a workbench. Foldable ones that are made of either aluminum, steel, or plastic are easy to store when you don't need them. Some have a shelf underneath to hold important tools.

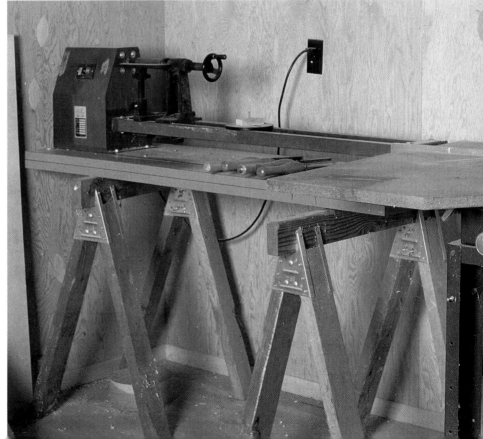

A sturdy permanent workbench made of plywood can easily handle larger projects, top right.

Saw horses are light enough to move around and can be the foundation for a work surface in a pinch, right.

Workbench Surfaces

THE TYPE OF WORKBENCH SURFACE you choose depends on the kind of work you'll be doing. Here are six common surfaces:

- **Plastic laminate** can withstand abuse and is ideal for most applications. It is resistant to many common chemicals and cleans up easily.
- **Laminated maple** is one of the strongest and most durable surfaces on which to work and can hold extreme weight.

> **» TIP** Some people say the ideal bench height is the distance between the floor and your hand (arm down, palm horizontal). But depending on your height, strength, and work style, your bench could be anywhere between 30 and 39 inches tall. Try several working heights before deciding what's best for you.

- **Hardboard** is a synthetic surface that is hard and durable. It resists many chemicals and will not warp or splinter.
- **Phenolic board** is a resin-impregnated, formaldehyde-free material that provides a 40-percent harder work surface than laminated hardwood.
- **Steel** stands up to banging, cutting, and general abuse, as well as motor oil and many chemicals.
- **Graphite composite** is lightweight, sturdy, and doesn't warp or splinter. It resists most chemicals—including oils and solvents—abrasion, corrosion, and moisture.

Workbench manufacturers offer work surfaces to accommodate the job you'll be doing. Some resist chemicals while others can handle extreme weight, below.

While laminated maple, opposite, is one of the strongest workbench surfaces, a high-pressure laminate top over a particleboard core is hard and durable.

STORAGE: A PLACE FOR EVERYTHING

A WOODWORKER OR MECHANIC needs other surfaces and work centers at his fingertips in order to finish a project. Well-planned storage can help you keep your workshop organized, help you find a tool when you need it, and equally important, free up countertop and workbench space. Details can make a big difference. Simple features, such as drawer dividers, will keep small items from becoming lost, and a rubber liner can prevent tools from sliding around and becoming mixed up when the drawers are opened and closed.

A rolling cabinet cart, below, provides storage for tools and frees up worktop space.

Outfit a wall storage system with hooks and plastic cubbies to hold tools, tape, and wire, opposite.

Adjustable wall-mounted shelving is a staple for workshops. You can remove and reposition the brackets to adjust the height of the shelves to suit your changing needs. Floor-standing shelves can also handle some of the storage load.

Rolling cabinet carts can be moved around in an auto or woodworking shop to fit your needs. Made of wood or metal, the cabinet's top provides a small but handy work surface while the base holds small power tools and supplies behind the cabinet doors.

Equipment carts made of metal or plastic come with wheels and can hold heavy or cumbersome items in one compact, mobile unit. You can use these carts to move equipment that you keep in a closet or a corner to the workbench.

Peg-Board panel can be installed instead of or directly over wallboard, giving you lots of space to hang dozens of hand tools. Peg-Board nailed to the wall and outfitted with all manner of hooks, loops, and racks is a flexible system for storing tools large and small. Group similar tools together so you can find them quickly. Peg-Board can also be painted a light a color to enhance lighting in the workshop.

Drawing each tool's outline on the wall behind its space is a classic and efficient way to keep track of where each tool belongs on the wall (or inside a tool cabinet). Spotting an unfilled outline will quickly tell you when a tool is missing.

ONE MORE THING ...

Sharp Thinking

THE INTERNET is a great source of more ideas for safely storing everything from chisels to knives to saw blades.

Cabinets

PLAN A COMBINATION of stationary and mobile cabinets on casters, which can be moved around the shop as necessary and stored underneath a workbench when not in use. Many contain pullout shelves that make it easy to see and reach tools at both the front and rear of each shelf. Tall storage cabinets are ideal for storing larger power hand tools and similar items.

Some cabinets are designed to hang on the wall. A slat-wall system uses composite panels that are simply fastened to the walls. The composite panels are easy to install and are designed to withstand heat, cold, and humidity. Once the weight-bearing wall panels are in place, you can hang modular cabinets by placing the preattached hooks into the slat and locking them into place. The panels also accommodate other items such as baskets, shelves, and even some tools.

If you're remodeling the kitchen soon, save and recycle the old cabinets to outfit your shop. Or, you could check out discontinued—and often discounted—lines at the local home-improvement store. Some of the cabinets' optional interior storage features, such as rollout bins, pullout shelves, and drawer dividers, can be useful in the workshop, too.

There are a few additional accessories you should have to properly round out you workshop storage.

- **Toolbox.** The simplest place for tools is a portable tote or box. These keep your tools secure and at hand when working in a corner of the shop away from the workbench or laying underneath a car in an auto workshop. Remember that the more tools your box contains, the less portable it will be. Experiment first by putting all the tools you've selected into a sturdy cardboard box and try lifting it.
- **Tool Caddy.** Made of high-impact plastic, a tool caddy is a revolving storage container that holds tools and items such as nails, bolts, screws, glue, and wire in tiers of circular trays.
- **Nail or Tool Pouch.** A nylon or leather pouch with pockets and compartments, this wearable storage pouch can hold fasteners and smaller tools.
- **Tool Belt.** Most tool belts are equipped with a steel or leather hammer loop, a measuring-tape compartment or clip, and various nail pouches and individual compartments for other tools. Made of leather or padded nylon for comfort, toll belts even have room for your cell phone.

Specialized storage racks can hold cleaning products, opposite left.

A row of rolling cabinets fit neatly under the workbench, opposite right.

Use plastic jars or containers to quickly find what you need, top left.

A convenient fold-down storage shelf often comes in handy, above.

A multi-drawer toolbox can hold a full array of tools for just about any job, left.

Storing Hazardous Chemicals

- Store flammable stains, varnishes, and finishes in metal containers. If possible, place them inside a ventilated metal cabinet that's well isolated from other flammables such as sawdust, papers, lumber.

- If you do store chemicals on a shelf, be sure it is above flood level. If your basement or garage floods, this will prevent contamination of the water.

- Place mineral spirits, turpentine, lacquer thinner, and denatured alcohol in metal safety cans with a spring-loaded cap and a flash arrestor that prevents ignited vapors from entering the can.

- Dispose of solvent-soaked rags properly and promptly—preferably outdoors where solvents will evaporate more easily. Never leave them lying around the shop.

- If stains, paints, or flammable chemicals are no longer usable, take them to a recycling center or a hazardous material collection site. Never pour them down a drain or into the toilet.

Flammable products should always be stored in a ventilated metal cabinet away from paper and lumber. Paints, thinners, and stains that you're no longer using should be properly recycled.

SAFETY

ONE OF THE MOST IMPORTANT THINGS to plan for in a workshop is safety. Always keep a first-aid kit in your workshop, and know where it is at all times. When you're using power tools, wear plastic goggles or safety glasses. Leave the goggles in a highly visible location—such as on the table of a drill press—as a reminder to wear them.

In addition to your eyes, protect your ears. Wear headphone-style ear protectors or at least ear plugs when you're using high-decibel power tools such as table saws and circular saws. Save your lungs, too, by wearing a protective respirator or dust mask to avoid breathing dust and other particulate pollutants.

Don't forget to install a smoke and carbon monoxide detector as well as a fire extinguisher in the workshop, and locate your circuit-breaker box where it's easiest to reach.

Finally, make sure to always have a phone, either a land line or a mobile device, on hand in case of an emergency.

Back-Saving Storage Solutions

FOLLOW THE SUGGESTIONS below to protect your back while working around a workshop—and always remember to bend your knees when lifting something that is stored on a low-lying shelf.

Height of shelf or cabinet above the floor	Recommended maximum weight of box or stored item at that height
64 in.–74. in.	10 lbs.
45 in.–64 in.	25 lbs.
29 in.–45 in.	50 lbs.
10 in.–29 in.	25 lbs.
6 in.–15 in.	15 lbs.

ONE MORE THING ...

STORE SHARP TOOLS in a drawer, never on a high shelf from which they can possibly fall and seriously injure you.

This homemade wood workbench not only includes plenty of built-in storage drawers but is also portable.

LIGHTING THE WORKSHOP

TO SEE BEST, you need to illuminate your workshop with the right intensity and type of light. If the light is inadequate, you'll strain to discern detail and color. If the light is too bright, you'll be blinded by the glare, which causes eyestrain.

General (overall) lighting, from both natural and artificial sources, provides the bulk of illumination in a workshop. Task lighting supplements general lighting when you need extra illumination for detail work.

A garage can be easily transformed into a workshop. It provides lots of space, a concrete slab for heavy equipment, and access for bulky items.

General Lighting

You'll want the best general light at machines, workbenches, and assembly areas. Corridors and storage areas require less illumination.

Windows not only let in natural light but also provide ventilation and prevent noise from power tools from leaking to the outside. To avoid glare and eyestrain, position the workbench so that natural light comes from behind you or from your side.

You might be able to upgrade natural lighting in the workshop with skylights. Install skylights on the north- or east-facing side of the roof to avoid

hot, direct sunlight that casts harsh shadows.

Fluorescents are usually a good choice for overhead lighting. They are inexpensive, easy to install, energy efficient, and they put out a lot of light, casting an even glow over the entire workshop. However, you'll need more than adequate general lighting—typically fluorescent tube lights—in a workshop. Directional (task) lighting—the type that can be focused on a drill press, for example—or stand lighting for working on your motorcycle will make detailed jobs easier and safer. Under-cabinet lighting may be helpful when you're working on some tasks at the workbench or on the counter. But make sure the light does not produce glare, which can cause eyestrain. You should be able to find what you need at any home-improvement store.

Portable, standing flood lights are handy for specific jobs, especially in an auto workshop. Directional, height-adjustable, and bright, they are ideal for focusing light in awkward places. A gooseneck lamp with a magnetic base is a good choice because it will stay put on any metal surface. You can move it as needed.

Fixtures

Track lighting is another good choice for overhead illumination and is best suited for focusing on a particular spot in the workshop. Flood lights can be used to brighten larger areas, while eyeball spotlights can focus concentrated light on smaller spaces. An advantage to any of these is that the individual fixtures can be directed toward a specific work area.

If you will be installing overhead fixtures, make sure they are on a separate circuit from the wall outlet. This way, the lights will remain on if a power overload from a tool trips a circuit breaker.

ONE MORE THING ...

Light Choices

INCANDESCENT AND HALOGEN light bulbs make things look slightly more pink than they appear in sunlight.

Fluorescent light bulbs make things look more blue or green than natural sunlight. Newer fluorescent bulbs on the market create light much closer to daylight. Because they are more energy efficient and last longer, they're a smart choice.

The new generation of compact fluorescent bulbs will help cut your energy bills while putting out plenty of light.

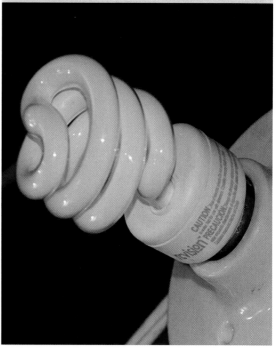

Many workbench manufacturers also make matching cabinets and storage solutions to produce a coordinated look, left.

VENTILATION

IT'S IMPORTANT to remove stale, musty air and replace it with cool, fresh air. Proper ventilation also gets rid of fumes from paints, adhesives, solvents, and other chemicals, as well as any smoke generated from welding or soldering or from wood that has been scorched during sawing. For good ventilation, your workshop should have at least two windows, or one window and a built-in exhaust fan.

When you're working with paints or finishes, the most effective way to vent the fumes is to place the piece you're working on between a fan that's exhausting air to the outside and an open door or window behind you to let in fresh air. Limit toxic fumes in the workshop by using low-VOC (volatile organic compounds) caulks, sealants, adhesives, and paints.

When you're working with wood, always wear a dust mask or respirator with a filter specifically for wood dust and be sure it seals properly over your mouth and nose. Dust helmets provide thorough protection for users with severe allergies to wood.

In an auto or motorcycle workshop, exhaust fans won't provide sufficient ventilation to move fumes from a running engine to the outside. Always connect a flexible hose to the exhaust pipe and pass it directly outdoors through a hose port in the door, or a permanently installed wall port located well away from any doors or windows to prevent reentry of the exhaust fumes.

If you're working with wood, think about adding a cutting or painting workstation that is apart from the workbench.

Types of Fans

FANS ARE NOT ONLY A GOOD WAY to cool a workshop and keep it from getting stuffy but can also be effective at moving fumes and fine sawdust generated during sanding. There are several basic types.

- **Industrial** fans can move large amounts of air and are especially good for a large shop.
- **Oscillating** fans move back and forth to enhance circulation. These won't get rid of chemical fumes, just blow them around.
- **Exhaust** fans installed into a basement or garage wall or an attic roof move fumes and stale air out of the workshop and to the outside.
- **Box** fans, which are inexpensive and portable, can be set up in a window to bring in outside air or turned around to draw out stale air.
- **Enclosed** fans, teamed up with air filters, can be installed in ductwork to suck out dirty air and return filtered air into the workspace.
- In an attic workshop, install an **attic ventilator** in the roof. Ventilators with a thermostatically controlled electric fan are good for large attic spaces. For smaller shops, a simple passive turbine ventilator is often adequate.

» TIP Locating a fan on the opposite side of an open window or door encourages flow-through ventilation.

CHAPTER 3

MEDIA AND GAME ROOMS

E VERY GUY NEEDS A GETAWAY. FOR SOME, IT'S THE HOME WORKSHOP TUCKED AWAY IN A BASEMENT OR GARAGE. FOR OTHERS, IT'S THE OUTDOOR KITCHEN, WHERE THEY CAN PRESIDE OVER THE GRILLING, SMOKING, AND BARBE-CUING. FOR MOST, IT IS PROBABLY THE MODERN MEDIA OR GAME ROOM, WHERE YOU CAN PLAY AN ACTION-PACKED VIDEO OR COMPUTER GAME, SHOOT SOME POOL AFTER A HARD DAY'S WORK, OR WATCH FOOTBALL OR A JUST-RELEASED DVD IN YOUR HOME THEATER. WHERE DO YOU LOOK TO CREATE SUCH A HIDEAWAY? IN A CORNER OF THE BASEMENT, AN ATTIC, OR EVEN THE BEDROOM OF A COLLEGE-BOUND SON. THE ONLY THING YOU NEED NOW IS A LITTLE GUIDANCE ON HOW TO DESIGN IT, FURNISH IT, AND EQUIP IT.

PREPARING THE ROOM

WITHOUT A PROPERLY OUTFITTED ROOM, even the most-expensive equipment won't sound its best. For those with a large budget, thick concrete walls with no windows, solid-core doors with yards of weather stripping, and sound-absorbing baffles on the walls and ceiling will result in a media room your friends will envy. But you can create something great on a small budget, too. Start with a rectangular room with as few doors and windows as possible. Open floor plans and vaulted ceilings make it more difficult to keep the sound effects in and don't block noise coming from outside the room. Any windows should be covered with thick or even motorized curtains that close with the push of a button on your remote. Too much light from a window increases screen glare and reduces contrast. On the other hand, staring at a brightly lit screen in an otherwise dark room will eventually strain your eyes. Dimmers on light-ing fixtures will help you find a happy medium.

Creating a media room, whether it be in the basement or a spare bedroom, means hooking up more than electronics. You'll need proper housing for all of the components, as well as comfortable furnishings. You can go the custom route, or check out the specialty cabinetry that's on the market. Manufacturers also design movie-theater-style row seating complete with cup holders and reclin-ing cushions, and floor-to-ceiling soundproofing systems that help to enhance the rich sound from digital equipment.

When it comes to furniture, the main focus should be on functionality that enhances your comfort and the entertainment experience. You can achieve both by furnishing the room with chairs, sectionals, or sofas that are upholstered in soft fabrics. Upholstery absorbs sound, as do throw pillows, and can provide the comfort level you need when watching a two-hour movie or playing the latest video game.

This game room, right, doubles as a hobby room with a wall of storage space to show off your favorite items.

Wraparound display cases, opposite bottom, transform this sleek, modern music room into a personal museum.

get wired

《 Make the Connection
Equip your room with the proper receptacles. This combination model, left, provides a central location for two grounded electrical outlets and inserts for a phone line and a coaxial cable.

》 TIP Remember to shut off the electricity at the main panel before doing any type of electrical project.

Cabinetry and Storage

YOU'LL NEED VARIOUS COMPONENTS, such as a DVD player, CD player, and so forth. Then there's the space that will house your growing collection of DVDs, Blu-ray discs, CDs, video-game cartridges, computer games, and remote controls. If you plan to order custom cabinetry for the space, buy your sound system and home-theater components first; then have the cabinetmaker design the unit to fit the equipment.

In terms of design, the cabinetry should accommodate components at eye level for easy operation. The topmost and lowest shelves can be reserved for lesser-used items. If you'll build the cabinet yourself, remember that there should be enough "breathing" space around the components—built-in electronics need ventilation. Plus, you have to leave space in the back for wires and plugs, and openings to pull through any cords that have to be plugged into wall outlets. Shelving that swivels out for easy access to the components is also a good idea, as is cabinetry with extra convenience features, such as interior lights and cooling fans.

In addition, be sure to include plenty of rollout drawers in the design to hold your library of favorite movies, music, and games. Closed cabinets are great for storing video games, while freestanding tower units keep music and movies organized and accessible. Or consider wall-mounted racks if floor space is at a premium. Some wall units are designed in attractive geometric shapes and make any collection of CDs or DVDs look like a work of art. Leave room for future purchases, too. Another option is to store tapes in a closet, a handsome trunk, or even a basket. Stockpiling DVDs, CDs, video games, and other clutter around the TV can detract from the viewing experience.

If you want to keep your music, video-game, and movie collection safe from prying eyes and sticky fingers, consider storing your collection in a cabinet that locks. Most have adjustable shelves and offset hinge points allowing 180-degree movement for better display and access to door storage.

When not in use, large TV monitors can look like bulky boxes. Hide modest-size TVs—27- or 32-inch models—behind the handsome doors of a semicustom cabinet. Large screens should probably be housed behind pocket, tambour, or concealed doors because oversize cabinet doors that swing out into the room can obstruct traffic or even your view of the screen. However, most people today prefer the sleek look of plasma and LCD TVs with monitors that are only a few inches thick. Their sleek design allows you to enjoy big-screen theater without sacrificing a lot of space. To save even more space, hang the monitor on the wall.

Custom-built shelving, opposite left, creates ample space for a DVD or video-game collection.

Curvilinear cabinets, opposite right, add eye appeal while housing a television and home-theater components.

This media room, above, uses custom cabinetry to stylishly integrate a home theater into the space.

ONE MORE THING ...

Retrofitting an Antique

AN ANTIQUE ARMOIRE may be handsome, but it was intended for linens or clothing, and it is not proper for housing media equipment.

MEDIA-WISE MOVES

NO MATTER THE SIZE of your budget or the physical dimensions of your space, there is a full range of options that will make a media/game room look as good as it sounds. You don't necessarily have to hire a professional or be one yourself to make design decisions that will enhance the space and your use of it.

Lighting

Figure out the purpose of the media room when considering lighting choices: is it just to view movies, or will you set up a computer to do office work at home and play computer games? Will you also use it as a reading room and to play Friday-night poker with friends? Then you will want a blend of ambient and task lighting. Rather than one or two bright-light sources, install several low-level lights. Dimmers will allow you to adjust lights for comfortably viewing a DVD or computer screen, or for reading or close-up work. Track lighting allows you to direct the light exactly where you want it. You can even install systems that provide custom lighting, creating the perfect setting at the touch of a button. As a general rule, no light should be brighter than the TV screen. Indirect illumination that provides ambient light without on-screen glare is best for a media room. To avoid eyestrain, position light sources behind you and not between you and the screen. Even if you don't consciously notice it, glare causes fatigue as your eyes strain to compensate. Remove the glare by turning off the television and checking for any reflections you see in the screen.

Ample seating and light-blocking curtains, below, create the perfect room for viewing movies.

A ventless fireplace, opposite top, adds extra warmth to this cozy media room.

Tall shelving, opposite bottom, provides easy access to DVDs or CDs.

> **»TIP** Lamps in a media room should have black or dark, opaque lampshades that direct light up and down. Translucent shades radiate light in all directions.

ONE MORE THING...

ODD-SHAPED ROOMS—those with more than four walls and an alcove—hold on to sound better than a space with four walls. But if your media room is like most, it's rectilinear. So, is there something you can do to compensate for this?

One easy way to accomplish the same effect is by including bookcases of different widths and lengths in the media room. Books help to cut down on echo, and you can arrange freestanding bookcases to break up an evenly dimensioned room—10 x 12 feet or 12 x 14 feet, for example—into an oddly dimensioned space, which provides a richer, more realistic sound.

Color and Light. Colored walls will reflect sunlight or artificial light and increase glare, both of which can wash out a television or computer screen. For the same reason, mirrors and other shiny materials or glossy finishes in a media room don't make sense. A wood coffee table with a low-luster finish and upholstered seating are better than hard composite materials. The same goes for artwork on the walls. If possible, don't frame paintings and posters in glass, which will dilute the rich sound coming from your expensive speakers. Choose deep neutrals such as mocha or cappuccino for walls, or even try a darker tone. Walls lined with corkboard, upholstered in fabric, or outfitted with high-tech sound-absorbing glass-fiber panels covered in fashionable fabrics are all good options.

These windows offer a handsome view, but they will need covering for watching TV without glare.

Sound Advice

ACOUSTICAL CEILING TILE is a simple and effective solution to prevent sound from leaking into other living areas. It comes in a range of styles, one of which is bound to coordinate with your decor. Double the tiles' soundproofing properties by first installing fiberglass batts between floor joists.

Carpeting is not only easy on the feet but also on the ear, preventing harsh echoes from bouncing around the room. Hard floor surfaces, such as tile, stone, and marble, can echo and distort the sound coming from even the most expensive receiver and speakers. Cover the floor in a low-pile, low-maintenance Berber, sisal, or industrial carpet to keep sound true and pure. Manufacturers also make static-free carpets so you can avoid those annoying shocks in wintertime.

When it comes to installing an entry door in the media room, some designers recommend a thick, insulated exterior-grade door to keep sound from leaking out. They also suggest an ample-size entryway so that furniture and large equipment can be brought in easily.

Ideally, placing speakers the right distance from the seating area—about 10 ft.—and no more than 5 ft. apart will create the optimum listening experience.

ONE MORE THING ...

THE MEDIA ROOM is not the place for overblown floral prints on fabrics or wallpaper. Nor is it a room that should have a lot of knickknacks. Clutter makes it difficult to focus on the picture, whether it be the latest movie on DVD or a video-game favorite. Keep the decorating simple. Create a muted solid-color or small-print background, and eliminate distractions.

A room without windows and the ability to dim the lighting replicates movie-theater ambiance.

CHAPTER 3: MEDIA & GAME ROOMS

PLUGGING INTO YOUR TV OPTIONS

TECHNOLOGY has clearly taken TV viewing to the next level. There are two things—at minimum—to pay attention to when buying a television: shape and size. To watch movies in their original widescreen format, you'll need a monitor with a rectangular shape 16:9 aspect ratio rather than the traditional, almost square 4:3. Size-wise, go for the largest screen you can afford—27 inches is probably the bare minimum. For optimal viewing, the distance between the viewer and the screen should equal about three times the screen size. So a 40-inch TV is best viewed from a distance of 10 feet (120 inches). Figure out where the seating will be located and calculate screen size accordingly. The display should be front and center, not off to one side, and at eye level.

If you want to make your media room a true home theater, you'll want to incorporate as much sophisticated equipment as possible. That includes speakers that can support surround sound and a high-definition television (HDTV).

HDTV is a digital signal that carries a detailed image and is encoded with surround-sound information. HDTV has twice the picture clarity of the old standard TV, whether you're watching a live broadcast or viewing a DVD.

For movie-theater realism, look for an HGTV with built-in 3-D capabilities and, provided you pair it with a high-definition DVD player, it will automatically switch to 3-D mode when it "knows" that a movie is in 3-D.

A professionally designed home theater, below left, replicates a movie-theater experience.

Play pool while watching the game in this rustic loft area, below right.

Flat-screens eliminate the distortion that plagued the curved edges of old models, and most can display the widescreen formats of DVDs. The tubes become too long and heavy to make manufacturing sets larger than 40 inches practical.

Plasma and LCD TVs are a mere 3 to 5 inches deep. Thin TV is a trend that is here to stay. Slimmed-down, flat-screen plasma TVs and LCD screens provide brilliant colors, better contrast and resolution, and greater viewing angle. Because the screen is flat, there is no problem with glare. Lighting does not affect the picture.

Plasma and LCD TVs come in a wide range of widths; 37 to 42 inches are the most popular for the residential market, but you can buy a 60-inch model if you have the space. Have *lots* of space? Consider a whopping 105-inch "TV wall."

Rear-projection TVs can have large cabinets— take note if you're planning on moving one into your basement, for example. The screen size can be as much as 82 inches and can been viewed in natural light without sacrificing picture quality. But you must watch rear-projection TV at eye level and straight-on for optimal viewing. Also make sure it can interface with satellite receivers, cable boxes, and HDTV DVD players.

Front-projection systems have a separate screen, which can either drop down from the ceiling or remain fixed on the wall, and a projector that is mounted at ceiling height across the room from the screen. It's akin to a movie-theater system. Front projection is expensive and requires a professional to install it. The image quality is unbeatable *if the room is dark.*

Sound-absorbing ceiling tile, carpeting, and a simple scheme transformed this basement into a comfortable getaway.

Speakers

TO REPRODUCE THE AUTHENTIC CINEMA EXPERIENCE at home, you need not only the visual components but also the audio ones—typically five speakers and one subwoofer. This setup is based on the Dolby Digital 5.1 technology, which breaks down the audio into six channels, each intended for a separate speaker.

Wattage is a good indicator of how loud a speaker can play without distortion. Choose speakers that are closely matched to your receiver's watts-per-channel rating. Don't worry about small differences in wattage; to double volume, you need ten—not two—times the power.

» TIP Speakers sound better when they're raised on stands or mounted on the wall rather than set atop bookshelves or cabinets.

You can rock out without disturbing the family in this well-insulated music studio, above.

Comfortable leather seating, dark paneling, and a professional projector and screen provide a true cinematic experience, below.

DVD Players and DVRs

HDTV DVD PLAYERS ARE AT THE HEART of today's home-theater systems. It's worth spending a little more on a progressive-scan DVD player. Unlike traditional players, which first paints every other line on the screen and then goes back and fills in the rest, progressive-scan paints them all at once, making for a smoother picture. If you don't want an intermission during multiple-disc movies, get a player with a disc changer.

For the sharpest picture, choose a player with component video (a trio of red, green, and blue RCA jacks) or S-video (a round jack with four pinholes) outputs rather than lower quality composite video (a single yellow RCA jack).

Digital video recorders (DVRs) record real-time programming from broadcast, cable, or satellite dish onto a hard drive; you can pause and rewind at any point. A DVR can be a stand-alone device or an extension of your cable or satellite service. Some DVRs have online capability, too.

An ornately carved pool table is a handsome counterpoint to the state-of-the-art plasma TV.

Remote Controls

Remote controls have become surprisingly advanced—you can spend thousands of dollars on a voice-activated remote that will dim the lights, start the movie, and fire up the popcorn maker with a touch of a finger. But there are also less-expensive devices that can cut down on coffee-table clutter. Whichever remote you choose, remember that an illuminated keypad or backlit screen will make it easier to operate in low-light situations.

You'll need the right wire and cable to hook up all of your home-theater components. The key to a good cable is its ability to insulate the signal it carries from interference, so buy the best-shielded ones you can afford. For video cables, choose those rated at 75 ohms, a necessity for transmitting HDTV signals smoothly. Avoid bundling wires and cables or placing them near power cords—both practices will increase interference and diminish signal quality. For speaker wire, if aesthetics are as much of a concern as performance, consider flat speaker wire, which is as thin as a credit card and can be mounted on walls. You can camouflage it with paint or wallcovering.

If acquiring all of the components individually seems like too much of a hassle, you can always keep it simple and pick up a home-theater-in-a-box. You'll get almost everything for a basic setup. Just unpack it and plug in the cord. One downside: depending on how integrated the system is, you may have to throw out everything later when you want to upgrade just the DVD player.

Control light, sound, and the movie from your seat with a built-in remote control, opposite.

ONE MORE THING...

WHEN STACKING YOUR GEAR, make sure there's at least 8 inches between the back of the components and the wall or rear of the cabinet to allow for easy installation, servicing, and ventilation. Receivers generate the most heat, so they need to go on top of the stack or on their own shelf with at least 2 inches of head room and a clear path for heat to escape. Don't forget that components that are housed in cabinets need ventilation, too.

Built-in audio and video components make for a neat and seamless look.

GAME ROOMS

A MEDIA ROOM can function as a home movie theater or as an entertainment center that allows you to play poker or pool with your buddies and pinball and board games with your family. Make sure you take time in the planning stages. You'll need to decide how much space you have to devote to it and what kinds of games you want to put in it.

There are many options these days; you aren't limited to just a pool table or dart board. Game-room furnishings have expanded over the years. Consider installing a bar or a jukebox and different types of games, such as foosball or ping pong.

Factor in ample square footage when designing a billiard room, below.

A redesigned basement, right, is a perfect space to locate an elaborate game room.

Pool and Game Tables

If you're planning on a pool table or game table as the central piece of furniture, check the measurements of the space first. Standard sizes of billiard tables range from 44 x 88 inches for an 8-foot table from bumper to bumper, to 56 x 112 inches for a 10-foot table. That's just the playing surface. Add onto that the length of the pool stick (48–52 inches), plus 6 inches for the stroke. Using that formula, the ideal room size for a game table would be approximately 14 x 18 feet.

Many pool-table manufacturers have matching accessories for the table, including bars, spectator chairs, game-table chairs, pub tables, and a matching entertainment center for a television and video-game console. Pool tables themselves come in many styles, including European, traditional, Arts and Crafts, casual, transitional, and competition. If your space is limited, you might want to try two-in-one or three-in-one tables. The *two-in-one* is a pool table with a reversible top so it can serve as a dining table or card table. The *three-in-one* includes bumper pool in its base. In addition, the dining side of the table can be inlaid with chess or backgammon boards. Or you can opt instead for a smaller foosball table or air hockey game.

Pool tables vary in price. At the lower end, there are mass-market, assemble-it-yourself tables for under $1,000. At the high end, professional tables can run into five figures.

High ceilings and modern furnishings create a sleek space for gaming or viewing a favorite movie, top left.

Generous lighting and built-in seating strike an inviting chord, left.

A mahogany pool table blends handsomely into this elegant paneled room, opposite.

Poker and Other Games

If you're looking for a card table for your weekend poker game, manufacturers provide almost unlimited options. If you want limited space, there is a range of full-size portable tables with room for up to eight to 10 players. When you're done, just fold it up and store it in a closet. If you want the table to be the center of attention, card tables come in a variety of configurations and materials. Formal pedestal card tables are designed in oak, cherry, and a variety of hardwoods and have a leather playing surface. Some come with a poker chip well and cup holders, along with matching chairs or genuine leather club chairs.

If your gaming preferences go beyond Texas Holdem, some game tables offer you the chance to try your luck at a variety of games. These casino tables allow you to play roulette, craps, checkers, chess, backgammon, and poker simply by flipping the table top. They also contain storage compartments for chips, game pieces, and other paraphernalia.

This multipurpose game room, below left, packs in everything from poker to pinball machines.

Any table and comfortable chairs, opposite, can be set up for playing board games.

ONE MORE THING...

IF CHILDREN PLAY in the game room, make it safe and install an electronic dartboard (that doesn't have sharp-tipped darts) rather than the real thing.

Video Games and Arcades

YOU CAN DEVOTE YOUR ENTIRE GAME ROOM to a video-game parlor or carve out a corner in your media room. It depends on your passions and your budget. Some of the same rules apply. If you like to play video games loud—and who doesn't—soundproof walls and carpeted floors will keep the noise from leaking into other parts of the house. Lighting is also key: you don't want to wash out the vibrant colors of your favorite game with too much light or glare. Putting lights on a dimmer and using window treatments can help you achieve a happy medium.

You can furnish your room with comfy beanbag chairs or specially made gaming chairs that you can connect to your TV's audio-out port for sound you can feel from head to toe. Some models have a subwoofer in the seat and two speakers atop the backrest so you can feel the sound. There is even a cupholder for your favorite refreshment in case you get thirsty.

Ventilation is always important when you have two or three PCs running along with a video-game console. An overhead fan will do the trick. Also, take a minute to add up your room's total power consumption, making sure your circuit can support it. High-performance PCs consume about 5 to 7 amps each; don't put more than two on a 15-amp circuit.

Creating an arcade space, complete with pinball machines and other arcade games, has never been easier. Every possible game you remember playing on the boardwalk or in an old-fashioned arcade is available for home use these days. Manufacturers make game cabinets that contain 80 classic games and feature two controllers, a track ball, and a 25-inch monitor. One manufacturer even makes a video-arcade center, which uses a projector and PC combo to offer a video jukebox and home theater in one system.

To create true arcade ambiance, primary lighting should emanate from the games' screen and marquee. Strong overhead lighting can produce glare on the screen. Choose diffused, indirect, and colored lighting instead. If your kids will be joining you for a night of gaming, consider installing rubber floor tile.

An open floor plan, top left, combines arcade machines with a home gym.

A jukebox, bar, and memorabilia on the walls add ambiance to this large game room, left.

REFRESHMENT CENTERS

WHETHER IT'S POKER NIGHT, a video-game night with friends, or just watching the latest DVD with the family, you don't want to miss a moment. You can outfit your media or game room with all the conveniences of a kitchen. Manufacturers make beverage centers that may consist of a small, below-counter refrigerator, an ice maker, or a wine cooler. There are also compact refrigerators complete with freezers on the market, as well as small microwave ovens that take little space. They even come in fashionable fingerprint-free stainless steel. If you want to duplicate the movie-theater experience, there are popcorn machines that look like they came straight from your local cinema. Some are portable, allowing you to move them out of the way when you are entertaining a crowd.

You can also outfit your media room with a temperature-controlled beverage center that will chill your favorite wine or brew. Some come with a built-in beer tap and a separate compartment for snacks that can be kept at room temperature. Of course, if you're going to eat and sip, you'll want to have a bar sink and a home for the dishes and glasses. There are freestanding refreshment centers that include a cold-water sink, large-capacity storage drawers, a pullout trash container, even a slide-out cutting board for slicing fruit or if you're planning on more elaborate snacks.

Outfit your media or game room with a wine cooler and storage for snacks, below left.

This beverage center includes wine racks and a hot-and-cold-water sink, below right.

CHAPTER 4

GAME COURTS & HOME GYMS

T HESE DAYS, MANY GUYS ARE SUPPLEMENTING—OR TRADING IN—THEIR GYM AND COUNTRY-CLUB MEMBERSHIPS WITH A HOME GYM IN THE BASEMENT OR A PUTTING GREEN OR GAME COURT IN THE BACKYARD. THE CONVENIENCE AND ACCESSIBILITY OF PRACTICING YOUR SHORT GAME OR PLAYING A GAME OF TENNIS WITH FRIENDS WITHOUT HAVING TO SIGN UP FOR TIME ON THE PUBLIC COURTS CERTAINLY HAS ITS APPEAL. WHAT'S MORE, WORKING OUT ON A TREADMILL IN THE MORNING BEFORE WORK OR DOING SOME STRENGTH TRAINING AFTER WORK WITHOUT HAVING TO DRIVE ACROSS TOWN TO A CROWDED GYM GIVES YOU ONE LESS EXCUSE NOT TO STAY FIT AND TRIM.

PUTTING GREENS

IF PRACTICE MAKES PERFECT, then perfection can begin in your own backyard. Many homeowners these days are installing personal putting greens so that they can hone their golf skills without any of the distractions they might have at a golf course or park. Repetition in a relaxed setting—without interruptions—may well be the key in helping you perfect your golf technique.

There are some things to think about before installing a putting green. Consider the location carefully. If you're interested only in practicing your putting, you may want to install a green adjacent to the house. In that case, you may want to elevate the surface of the green slightly and border it with plants and architectural elements, such as Windsor blocks. If you also want to practice chipping and pitching, locating the green in an area away from the house probably makes sense. You might construct it so that the surface is at ground level surrounded by a simple berm. Consider the topography of your property, and select an area that will require the least amount of grading. To integrate the putting green into the landscape and create a focal point, use plants of varied color, texture, and height, along with large boulders and rocks.

Many dedicated golfers don't just install any putting green in their backyard. They commission designers to re-create world-famous greens designed by the likes of Robert Trent Jones and others so that they feel as if they're playing at Pebble Beach or Augusta. Virtually any type of green can be installed in your yard, as long as you have the space and the money for it.

If you are budget-conscious and handy, you can purchase a putting-green kit online. The kit contains synthetic turf, regulation cups, and a 30-inch pole with ball-trap disk and comes with step-by-step installation instructions. Sizes range from 12 x 12 to 12 x 108 feet.

A nifty "clubhouse" and handsome shrubbery frame this five-hole putting green, integrating it into the backyard landscape.

Natural versus Synthetic Turf

ASK YOURSELF: do you want a natural-grass putting green or one with artificial turf? While natural grass provides the truest roll, it requires year-round maintenance and is affected by the changing seasons. You have to mow, water, and fertilize the green. The new generation of artificial turf is weatherproof, UV-resistant, and usable any time of year. The only maintenance that is required is occasional sweeping to revitalize fibers. Rolling the surface with a water-filled lawn roller can increase speed and smoothness.

Synthetic turf is made of either nylon or polypropylene. Manufacturers produce it with specific playing characteristics. You can install turf with weaves that are perfect for putting and greenside shots of less than 10 yards or products tailor-made for longer shots of 175 yards.

The newest types of synthetic turf putt, bounce, and react to a shot very much like a natural-bent green grass. The green will hold a shot, and balls with backspin will stop or back up just as they do on grass. Most importantly, the new synthetic surfaces allow the ball to roll true and at an even pace, at fast or slow speeds.

Installing a putting green is an elaborate process that only a skilled contractor can do. The process requires excavation and compacting of the site and laying down a special fabric to stabilize the base. Then two layers of crushed stone are laid down, compacted, and contoured. Synthetic turf is placed, cut, and shaped. Finally, a special in-fill system, made of round quartz granules and colored-acrylic coating, is integrated into the turf to give it a naturally soft feel and a deep, rich luster similar to grass.

Adding a sand bunker into the putting-green design allows you to practice your pitch and wedge shots.

ONE MORE THING ...

TO GIVE THE SETTING for your putting green a natural look, avoid using straight lines or evenly shaped arrangements because exact symmetry doesn't occur in nature. Instead, outline the putting green in an irregular shape.

A synthetic green, below, requires minimal maintenance, won't fade from the sun, and can be played on year-round.

Putting Green Options

YOU CAN EQUIP YOUR GREEN with regulation PGA cups and flags. Lighting systems are also available that allow you to practice your short game at night. If you have room in your backyard, consider having a sand bunker installed to sharpen your pitching game. Or you can create a bunker yourself in one afternoon. Select a location surrounded by an adequate amount of lawn space to allow you to make chip shots. Using a hillside location, if there's one available, will allow you to chip down into an open area and will require less digging for the installation.

If you want to hone your long game, you can have a ball-retrieval system installed alongside the green. It is a self-contained green, complete with synthetic turf, that allows you to practice drives and other full-swing shots. The ball is caught by a special net at one end that is designed to roll the ball back to your feet. The system allows you to use one ball repeatedly.

This secluded backyard putting green, below, allows you to practice your short game in privacy.

Installing a putting green, opposite, is a complex process best left to an experienced contractor.

GAME COURTS

A DECADE AGO, homeowners had to make a choice: do I want a half-court basketball court, tennis court, or a volleyball court? These days new multisport designs allow you to play close to a dozen sports on one court. Lines are painted and inlaid into the court so that you can play everything from paddle tennis to shuffleboard. Installing this type of court has many benefits: it keeps children close to home, reduces the probability of injury with the new generation of easy-on-the-joint surfaces, and provides an excellent gathering place for family and friends if you entertain outdoors. Game courts come in a variety of shapes, sizes, and, unlike asphalt and concrete, colors to suit the needs of your family and your property. You can even personalize the court with the logo and colors of your favorite team or alma mater.

Unlike rigid asphalt and concrete surfaces, the new generation of game-court surfaces is made of interlocking polyethylene tiles that provide shock absorption to protect knees, ankles, and tender lower backs. The surface actually gives and gently pushes back when you run or move on it. Because they are custom built, outdoor game courts can be constructed to blend with any outdoor landscape. If your backyard can't accommodate a full-size basketball court, then a half-court might fit your space perfectly.

Game courts are also extremely durable. With minimal maintenance, a game court will not flake, blister, or crack due to water or extreme heat or cold. The court stays clean because its surface is self-draining, allowing water and dirt to escape. The synthetic tiles are designed to shed water and are ready to play on almost immediately after a hard rain. The court doesn't have to be resurfaced or repainted. Simply use a broom or leaf blower to remove debris—or hose off dirt. If a tile is damaged, it can easily be replaced by a contractor.

You can also retrofit an old court with a new surface. If you already have a tennis or basketball court that is in need of refurbishing, consider resurfacing it with high-performance, low-maintenance court material.

The new generation of game courts allows you to play everything from tennis to shuffleboard on one weather-resistant surface, right.

A chain-link fence—or new soft netting options that don't obstruct your view—prevents the ball from leaving the court, opposite top.

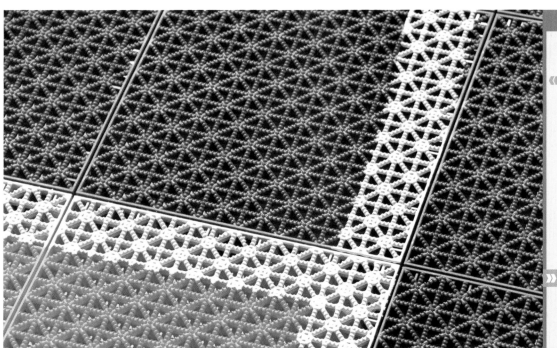

get started

« Find the Right Pro

When you're ready to install a game court, find a professional who is experienced and can work with your budget. If you see one in the neighborhood that you like, find out who did the job.

» TIP You can use game-court tiles for garage or basement floors or to create a unique deck or patio surface, too.

Game-Court Options

GAME-COURT MANUFACTURERS also make the options to complete the backyard court: hoops, goal systems, fences, netting, even courtside seating. You can prevent the ball from leaving the court with a standard chain-link fence or with new soft fencing options that use thin netting to keep errant shots from bouncing outside the court. The netting is almost invisible and doesn't obstruct the view of your yard.

A multiuse rebounder allows you to hone your tennis, badminton, and soccer shots without having to chase the ball. The 10-foot-high × 20-foot-wide net, framed by a coated-steel system, sends the ball back to you with truer velocity than any practice wall can. Unlike concrete practice walls, there is no noise to disturb family or neighbors. A multisport net-adjustment kit is a perfect addition for those who play a variety of net-based sports. Set it low to play tennis or paddleball or raise it to play badminton or volleyball. Lighting systems can be installed to illuminate an entire tennis court or simpler systems can be attached to a basketball backboard if you want to shoot hoops day and night.

You can easily adjust the net on this tennis court, which also allows you to play volleyball when you're in the mood.

Bocce and Horseshoe Courts

Bocce is second only to soccer in worldwide popularity, and increasingly homeowners are installing bocce-ball courts in their backyard or as part of an outdoor room. The game allows family and friends to have fun and stay active at a get-together or outdoor party without sweating or needing special equipment. International regulation courts are 91 feet long × 13 feet wide, but a court 60 feet × 10 feet is flexible for all levels of play. Bocce-ball courts are often installed by a contractor, but if you are handy, you can do it yourself. Side and back walls should be constructed of wood, preferably treated wood so that they resist rot. The surface should be relatively smooth and level. The bocce-ball court surface should also be hard-packed and made from a mixture of clay and oyster shell with a topping of oyster-shell flour. Limestone, brick dust, and decomposed granite are also acceptable surfaces. Fortunately, synthetic surfaces are being developed that minimize maintenance.

For those who don't have the room in their yards to construct their own bocce-ball court, manufacturers make portable ones that you can easily assemble. The kits come with vinyl front, back, and side walls that, when put together, create a 60 × 12-foot court on your lawn. When you're finished playing, take up the walls and store them for the next outing.

Horseshoes. Horseshoe courts have evolved beyond a rectangle of dirt with two metal stakes hammered into the ground. You can add pressure-treated wood pitching platforms, elaborate backstops, solar lighting, and landscape around the court to integrate it into the backyard. A regulation horseshoe court is at least 50 feet long × 10 feet wide and consists of two pitcher's boxes, each 6-feet square, with a stake in the center. Flanking them are two pitching platforms, from where horseshoes are thrown. The pitching distance is 40 feet for men, 30 feet for women. Install the court with a north-south orientation to minimize the effects of the sun from stake to stake. Clay, sand, dirt, and low-maintenance synthetic materials are all acceptable surfaces for the court.

If you're a casual player, buy a horseshoe set, hammer the stakes in the ground, and start pitching. Sets range in price. The best—drop-forged steel horseshoes sold with a solid-steel stake—are made expressly for the game and approved by the national association. The least-expensive sets have hard rubber horseshoes with two wooden pegs.

Bocce has become a popular game in the U.S. The court requires minimal space.

About Synthetic Surfaces

WHEN LANDSCAPE DESIGNER and builder Neil Christensen started installing multisport game courts and synthetic putting greens seven years ago, there was a curiosity about both products. "The trend has grown every year since then," says Christensen, whose business is located in Hillsdale, New Jersey. "These days, a day doesn't go by that we don't get a call about these products."

"It took a while for golfers to accept synthetic putting greens because they thought the turf was similar to Astroturf," says Christensen. "Nothing could be further from the truth. Today's synthetic-turf technology is light years better than old Astroturf. The new product has true roll, which means the ball rolls end over end and doesn't wobble on its way to the cup. Plus, the turf absorbs the force of the ball when you're hitting a shot from 200 yards out. It performs like real grass."

The new synthetic-turf putting-green systems are best installed by professionals. "A handy do-it-yourselfer is not going to get nearly the results from the green that a professional will," says Christensen, who not only installs putting greens but designs them as well. "You have to install a base, the turf, and an in-fill system, all of which need to be integrated in a precise way. Unless you get it right, you're going to compromise performance."

In the end, performance is everything to customers. "The clientele who have putting greens are smart and well educated," says Christensen, who has a 3 handicap. "They don't care how you build it, they just want it to perform like natural turf. And it does."

A basketball court easily converts into a roller-hockey rink with a quick installation of the lightweight goals.

HOME GYMS

If you're active, chances are your workouts don't stop on the court. In fact, they may begin, end, or happen entirely in the gym. Today you can set up your home gym anywhere you have the space, but many find that the basement or attached garage is a perfect spot for strength and cardio machines. Concrete-slab floors found in most basements and garages are a blessing and a curse. They can support heavy workout machines, but they are uncomfortable for long periods of standing. Whatever you put down should be able to take a lot of wear and tear. Vinyl or rubber tiles that are at least ⅜ inch thick are a practical and inexpensive option. They offer more protection and cushioning than a carpet and are maintenance free. (A few swipes of a damp rag will clean them.)

When planning a home gym, leave enough space between cardio and strength-training machines to avoid injury.

Ventilation and Light

PLANNING YOUR GYM in a section of the basement, garage, or another space with several operable windows serves two purposes: looking outside takes your mind off the workout and opening a window allows you to get fresh air in a room that can quickly get stuffy and stale. Window treatments, such as wooden shutters or blinds, will enable you to screen out the sun during the hot summer months. If windows aren't an option, arrange electrical outlets to include a large overhead fan. Standing oscillating fans can also take the heat off when you're doing a tough workout.

Track-mounted or recessed fixtures can direct supplemental lighting where it's needed without getting in your way as you exercise.

Neutrals and warm whites on the walls will make the gym feel brighter and more spacious, which can enhance your motivation. Lightweight, shatterproof-acrylic mirror panels on the walls will also reflect natural and ambient lighting and enable you to check out your form while strength training.

No matter what kind of exercise appeals to you, watching a game on TV, a favorite DVD, or tape makes the most strenuous exercise session go by more quickly. Be sure to upgrade and arrange wiring, cable, and receptacles. Integrate wiring from your media room into your gym layout so you can listen to music while working out. Flush-mounted speakers in the ceiling or speakers mounted in the four corners of the room provide rich sound without getting in the way of your gym equipment. If you spend a lot of time on the treadmill, fixing a TV on a swiveling, ceiling-mounted corner bracket allows you to view the set from anywhere in the room.

An open floor plan and large windows can transform a home gym into a more welcoming space.

ONE MORE THING ...

WHEN PLANNING SPACE for a home gym, factor in room between the machines to prevent banging your arms and legs during a workout. Experts agree that there should be a minimum of 30 inches between each piece of exercise equipment.

Mirrors give the feeling of added room to this gym where space is at a premium.

Gym Equipment

To accommodate your cardiovascular and strength-training needs, you will probably want one or two cardio machines and either a set of dumbbells or a weight-lifting station. A stationary bike remains an evergreen piece of equipment among home-gym enthusiasts because it takes up little space and can be used by those who suffer from knee, hip, lower back, or weight problems. Elliptical trainers and treadmills are the most popular cardio machines. Treadmills are perhaps the most versatile, allowing you to either walk or run on them. To prevent workout boredom, it is wise to have more than one type of machine in your gym.

In terms of strength training, you have two options: free weights (dumbbells and a bar and metal weights) or an all-in-one weight-lifting station with a bench. If you will be working out alone most of the time, the latter is probably the best

A blend of cardio and strength-training machines, along with free weights, is the foundation of a good home gym.

choice because you don't have to worry about being crushed under the bar if the weight is too heavy for you.

After a workout, nothing soothes sore muscles like a stint in a steam shower, sauna, whirlpool, or hot tub. If your home gym is in the basement or an attached garage, it makes good sense to install a hot tub, shower, or sauna in the same location. Plumbing and electrical service are centrally located and easily accessible there. In addition, the concrete-slab floor can support a hot tub filled with water or some of the new oversize whirlpool tubs without any structural reinforcement.

Whirlpool and Soaking Tubs. A whirlpool tub has jets that force out air or water to create a massaging effect. Many tubs offer jets that can be redirected to massage a sore neck or adjusted to increase or decrease pressure. However, you can't use bath oils or salts with a water-jetted system

because of the possibility of bacterial growth inside the jet tubes. But you can use aromatic oils in tubs with air systems. This type has 30 to 70 small holes drilled around the radius of the tub that emit soft, gentle bubbles. Some air-system tubs are also equipped with water jets.

Soaking tubs are deeper than, but not as long as, standard tubs. They allow you to submerge yourself comfortably in water up to your neck.

Spa Showers. If you don't have time to wait for an oversize tub to fill, think about a spa shower. Today's showerheads and sprays offer the massaging action of whirlpool jets as soon as you turn on the water. Some showerheads are positioned to hit the body first in case you don't want to get your hair wet. For a whole-body shower, try a rain dome—a wide-diameter head mounted on the ceiling that emits a large volume of water but a gentle flow. Or consider a shower tower: four to ten jets are positioned in a vertical column to reach every part of the body. Don't forget to equip your shower with a thermostatic valve, which allows you to preset the temperature.

A steam shower, which is tightly enclosed from the ceiling to the floor, has become extremely popular. It has a steam generator built into the shower wall. You can include an oversized bench in the design and a whirlpool foot bath that can be recessed into the shower floor.

Relaxing in a soaking tub made of stone, top right, is the perfect way to finish up a vigorous workout.

A swim spa, right, is a great way to get all the health benefits of swimming in a small space.

Saunas and Hot Tubs

WHO HASN'T HEADED TO THE SAUNA after an agonizing workout on the elliptical trainer or a heavy bout of strength training? It's a luxury many have thought about having in their own home. Saunas can be installed just about anywhere. Because they use dry heat, saunas don't require a water supply or drain. What's more, the sauna stove can be tied directly into existing household circuits.

The original Finnish sauna was a one-room log cabin heated with a woodstove. Today, there are multiple options limited only by the amount of space you have and your budget. Some saunas even incorporate dressing rooms, massage rooms, and cold-water plunges.

Prefab units, both compact and grand, come with doors, paneled walls, sauna stove, and all hardware. Larger versions include a bar and bedroom. Some saunas are made of cedar and provide a soothing fragrance when heated. Infrared saunas heat the body directly rather than circulating hot air throughout the enclosure.

Any time you install a sauna, include ventilation to take care of any condensation that might build up on the outside of the unit as well as extra insulation in the walls to provide energy efficiency.

Hot Tubs and Spas. Today's hot tub has a lining that is made of acrylic, thermoplastic, or soft vinyl, and its shell may come in a wide spectrum of colors and textures. A typical unit is 5 to 6 feet in diameter and has a depth of 3 to 4 feet.

Always wet-test a hot tub in the showroom to make sure it's comfortable and that the jets direct water where you want it. Also, make sure that you can reach the controls without leaving the water. Some models have integrated aroma-therapy systems, stereo systems with waterproof speakers, built-in TVs, and LED underwater lights that change color.

You can locate a compact sauna in a corner of a refinished garage, basement, or even a deluxe shed.

Sauna Etiquette and Safety

■ Remove jewelry, eyeglasses, and contact lenses. They may conduct heat in the sauna and burn you.

■ Don't enter with a full stomach. Allow a couple of hours between the sauna and meals.

■ Plan your time. Some people like to sauna after exercise to soothe sore muscles. Others prefer to sauna at the end of the day to bring on sleep.

■ Vary the heat and length of stay. Novices need to build up endurance. Children, for example, should stick their feet in a bucket of cool water to moderate the impact of the heat.

Saunas made of cedar, below, relax tight muscles while delivering a pleasant fragrance as they heat.

CHAPTER 5

GRILLING SPACES

F THERE IS A PROTOTYPICAL GUY'S SPACE, IT'S THE BARBECUE PIT OR GRILLING AREA. THESE DAYS IT COULD BE AN OUTDOOR KITCHEN. NO LONGER JUST A CHARCOAL HIBACHI, REDWOOD PICNIC TABLE, AND AN UMBRELLA, AN OUTDOOR KITCHEN HAS ALL THE AMENITIES OF ITS INDOOR COUNTERPART. IN FACT, THE OUTDOOR KITCHEN HAS BECOME AN EXTENSION OF THE HOME'S LIVING SPACE. AS A RESULT, OUTDOOR KITCHENS ARE OFTEN OUTFITTED WITH DELUXE APPLIANCES, WEATHER-RESISTANT CABINETRY, STONE COUNTERTOPS, LIGHTING, PLUMBING, AND, IN SOME CASES, OUTDOOR TV AND SOUND SYSTEMS. ON THE FOLLOWING PAGES, YOU WILL FIND IDEAS FOR EVERYTHING FROM WHERE TO CREATE AN OUTDOOR KITCHEN TO HOW TO TURN THE SPACE INTO A GRILLIN' GUY'S DREAM ROOM.

LOCATION, LOCATION

OUTDOOR KITCHENS are typically built on new or existing patios, decks, and pool areas for two reasons: to provide easy access to the house for ferrying food and supplies back and forth and to tie into existing utilities. Tapping into the house's gas, electrical, and plumbing lines is most practical when the outdoor kitchen is situated alongside the house or attached to a back wall. When you're planning to install built-in appliances, be sure to check local building and fire codes. Zoning laws may restrict size and location, and fire codes dictate clearance requirements between an open flame and a combustible surface.

Other popular places where you could plan to build an outdoor kitchen include an attached porch, a garage, a gazebo, or a pavilion. You can install a grilling station or a completely equipped outdoor kitchen just about anywhere, but if you don't want to have to extend the utilities, stick to a spot that is close to the house.

Outdoor kitchens can be as luxurious and well-equipped as their indoor counterparts. This rustic design with a panoramic view includes a stone fireplace, a hot- and cold-water sink, refrigerator, wine cooler, and a chandelier to light up the dining area.

Size, Height, and Shape

MANY FACTORS influence the size, height, and shape of an outdoor kitchen. Size, for example, is a function of the available space as well as the appliance dimensions and the number of people you plan to entertain. Height may be determined by whether or not you want to keep your outdoor kitchen on the same level as your indoor kitchen, by the view you'd like to see, or by safety issues. Terrain and landscape features often determine shape, but it also has a lot to do with style and aesthetics.

Most successful designs tend to blend with their surroundings. If you plan to build your entertainment area near the house, try extending the existing lines of exterior walls to create a unifying shape. If your house has a sunroom, use similar proportions for your outdoor-kitchen structure. If your kitchen will be away from the house, try to make it relate to an existing outbuilding or build it around a landscape feature, such as a garden bed. Remote cooking and dining areas can typically take on a more organic shape than outdoor kitchens built next to the house.

This pavilion looks like a deluxe barn, with a wood-fueled grilling pit as the focal point. Its design is not only open, taking full advantage of the beautiful views, but also practical, adding a generous amount of bench seating.

Convenient Access

You will also need to decide how you will access the outdoor kitchen from the house and yard. Patio doors are the most practical house-to-outdoor kitchen transitions. They afford a view of your entertainment area and yard from inside your house and come in a variety of configurations. Choose the widest door that will fit your plan. French doors also make roomy, graceful transitions. Adding a second door from the house to an outdoor entertainment area will take the pressure off a heavily trafficked back door.

Grills come in all sizes these days and include storage for cooking items and condiments.

Folding Walls

IF YOU HAVE LIMITED SPACE for your outdoor cooking and dining zone, consider a folding wall. It will allow you to share indoor and outdoor space as if it were one room. In effect, both spaces are expanded. Installed between an indoor kitchen and outdoor area, folding walls provide one really large cooking facility with everything at your fingertips. Similarly, you can double or triple the capacity of a dining room by opening it to the outside with a folding wall.

A folding wall allows the outdoor kitchen to instantly become part of the main house.

LANDSCAPING STRATEGIES

PLANTS, TREES, SHRUBS, WALLS, AND FENCES, as well as careful grading, can make the difference between an outdoor kitchen and entertainment area that sits well in the yard and one that's an eyesore. In general, use hedges and shrubs to "ground" cabinets and large built-ins, such as grills and walls. Use low plantings, such as flower beds, around your dining area or wherever you'd like to open the view. Vines grown on trellises are a good way to screen unwanted views and to create a sense of enclosure.

When designing the landscape around an outdoor kitchen or any outdoor living space, your aim should be to create interesting views not to screen out the yard. Unless privacy is an issue, plant trees and shrubs at varying distances from the dining area to create vistas with depth and interest. You can also make a small yard appear larger by planting several shrubs 10 or 15 yards from the deck or patio perimeter. Plant smaller specimens farther away from your deck or patio. Do the reverse to make your yard seem smaller and more secluded.

The slate path and decorative gravel ground this outdoor kitchen, while low plantings open the view.

Shelter Options

Houses with porches or deep eaves provide natural shelter for outdoor cooking and dining, but unless you're fortunate to have one, you're going to devise another solution. A roofed structure is the most permanent option and can often be designed to fit in with your home's architecture. Pavilions and gazebos are usually detached from the house. They can be screened or not. Detached structures are often pleasing focal points for the backyard landscape. They offer a sense of getting away from it all.

Creating Shade. Keeping a sunny outdoor living space cool during the hot months is no easy task, but creating some shade will definitely help. The simplest approach is a center-post umbrella that's designed to fit through a hole in a dining table into a base below it. If you go this route, buy a large umbrella that's 8 to 12 feet wide and easy to open and close. Side-post umbrellas get the post out of your way and come in even bigger sizes. The umbrellas mount on an arm or hang from a boom that can rotate 360 degrees to block the sun as it crosses the sky. Post-less umbrellas can be hung from an overhead structure, such as a sturdy arbor or pergola.

Other outdoor-room covering options include awnings and shade cloth. Awnings are either manually or electrically powered. They attach to your house and provide protection from both the sun and the rain. You can also stretch shade cloth over the area with cables or secure it over a structure, such as an arbor or pergola.

Freestanding gazebos, fitted with outdoor fabric, will offer respite from the sun. Shade sails, aptly named because they look like ships' sails, are an innovative way to add shade and contemporary styling to an outdoor dining area. Held together by stainless-steel cable sewn into the edges, the triangular or rectangular sails attach to posts or to the structure with steel rings at reinforced corners.

Handsome shade sails, opposite, are a stylish way to minimize the sun's rays while you're grilling.

A stylish hardwood overhang shelters this "kitchen garage," above. Stacked doors unfold to close off the area when it's not in use.

Several ceiling fans expel cooking fumes and cool down this large outdoor-kitchen pavilion.

Trellises and Arbors. Trellises, arbors, and other overhead shade structures can give your outdoor kitchen and dining area a lush, secluded feel while reducing glare and heat from the sun. Use trellises to create flowering walls that will shelter you from wind and sun. Use arbors to create outdoor ceilings laced with greenery. Be sure to design your arbor to carry the weight of heavy, vigorous vines, such as wisteria, trumpet vines, climbing hydrangea, and grape.

More Temperature-Control Options. To add heat, fireplaces and fire pits do a great job. They

add adventure and romance to the environs as well. If you want something a bit more conventional, consider a patio heater. Parasol-shaped models are the most popular because they can be moved. Find them at outdoor furniture stores and on various online shopping sites.

Besides ceiling fans in roofed enclosures, evaporative coolers, either installed behind a wall, or placed in the garden, can lower the temperature by as much as 10 to 30 degrees, depending on the conditions. Large, high-pressure misting fans can cool areas of 400 square feet and more.

The heater next to this sofa extends the enjoyment of the outdoors into the fall.

CHAPTER 5: GRILLING SPACES

GET COOKING

THE GRILL IS THE HEART of an outdoor kitchen—and it may end up being its most expensive component, too—so choosing the best one is an important decision. There are lots of options today. Here are some points to consider before you put down your hard-earned money.

A grill can either be *built-in* or *freestanding*. A grill that is built into a countertop or grill island usually has more cooking capacity and plenty of work area on each side. A freestanding unit on wheels, on the other hand, is better if you want to be able to move your grill, either to clear the area when you're not cooking or to move the grill to a more optimum position when the weather or season changes.

Grills come with a variety of options and add-ons, such as a side burner for making sauces and a warming rack, below.

If you often entertain large groups, consider a grill with at least a 600-sq.-ft. cooking area and perhaps a rotisserie, opposite.

Choosing the Right Grill

Determine the grill size that's right for you. Are you a weekend griller for a small family? If so, a surface area of 300 to 450 square inches should suffice; a larger family might require 450 to 600 square inches. If you host large parties, you'll need a cooking area of at least 600 square inches.

A Btu (British thermal unit) is the standard measurement for heat output, but it isn't always a true measure of a grill's cooking power. More important is the ability of a grill to reach and sustain cooking temperatures—and this depends on a number of factors, including size and heat distribution. In general, grills with two burners should produce 30,000 to 50,000 Btu, or about 100 Btu per square inch of cooking surface. Burners should spread heat evenly to the cooking surface.

Fuel Options for Grills

NATURAL GAS AND LIQUID PROPANE are by far the most popular choices. For flavor, however, many traditionalists won't go near a gas grill, instead favoring a charcoal unit. Electric grills and pellet grills are other options.

Gas. A gas grill is simply a grill that uses gas from a tank or a natural gas line for fuel. The grill is fueled by liquid propane or natural gas—not both. Liquid propane is typically stored in cylindrical tanks and is almost always located on a shelf below or hung on a bracket beside the grill. Natural gas-fueled grills do not require tanks, so the possibility of running out of gas during cooking is eliminated. They are permanently hooked up to your home's natural gas supply. Excluding installation costs, natural gas is about half the cost of propane to operate.

Charcoal. With a charcoal grill, the principal fuel is either natural-lump charcoal or charcoal briquettes (compacted ground charcoal, coal dust, and starch). Natural-lump charcoal burns hotter, which means you use less. Charcoal grills are the choice for purists who want to *barbecue* (a long, slow heating process), not *grill* (cook quickly directly over high heat). Charcoal grills come in many sizes: from hibachi to a kettle grill to a large powder-coated steel model. Built-in charcoal grills are not as readily available as their gas counterparts, but their number keeps rising.

Pellet. You might not have heard of pellet grills, but they are becoming increasingly popular. Small wood pellets provide the fuel source and infuse the food with flavor from the smoke. The pellets, which are stored in a hopper, are available in a variety of flavors, including mesquite, hickory, apple, and alder. They can be fed into the firebox at variable rates—slower for barbecuing and faster for grilling. Pellet grills are catching on thanks to their energy efficiency and their clean-burning properties.

Electric. These make up only a tiny fraction of the barbecue market, and they can be more difficult to find than the other types of grills, but they may be worth a look. Electric grills, available as built-in or freestanding units, are easy to operate and maintain. They are also ready to cook in the shortest amount of time. An electric grill is often smaller than its gas and charcoal counterparts, so it may be more suited for those living in an apartment or condominium. Many argue that the flavor an electric grill imparts doesn't come close to what a charcoal or gas model produces.

This charcoal grill, below left, uses a gas assist to light the coal fast.

Gas grills can be fueled by either liquid propane, below, or natural gas.

Grill Accessories

You've selected a grill. Now it's time to outfit it. If you want to turn your grill into a multifunctional cooking center, consider the following extras.

A *side burner* allows you to boil a pot of water for corn or lobster, heat sauces, or stir-fry vegetables, eliminating the need to run back inside again and again. A warming rack is just a shelf, often removable, located above the main cooking surface that keeps food warm.

For slow, even cooking, consider a *rotisserie*, which is a motorized spit (long metal rod) that suspends and slowly rotates food over the grate. The rotisserie is a popular grill accessory because it slowly roasts, creating foods crispy on the outside and tender and juicy on the inside. If you want to create flavorful foods without springing for a smoker, outfit your grill with a *smoker box*. These perforated metal containers hold wood chips, imparting a smoky flavor to your foods. Smoker boxes are located on a gas grill's lava rocks or ceramic briquettes, or on a charcoal grill's grate.

A *grill basket* is a must-have for fish or other fragile foods. A hinged wire basket with a latch allows you to flip the food with no mess, making searing your favorite filet incredibly easy.

A full complement of grilling utensils is a basic necessity, turning the chef into master of his outdoor kitchen, top right.

This built-in gas grill, was set into the outdoor kitchen's stone countertop, above right.

A high-quality charcoal grill has a thermometer built into the hood so that you can monitor a precise cooking temperature, right.

Beyond Grills

A GRILL ISN'T THE ONLY WAY to go when it comes to preparing meals in an outdoor kitchen. Depending on the types of foods you like to cook, here are some other options:

SMOKER

The main difference between a charcoal grill and a smoker is that a smoker keeps the fire away from the food. Water smokers include a heat source on the bottom, grilling racks on top, and a pan of water in between, creating a type of indirect cooking. Dry smokers burn small pieces of wood in a firebox and the cooking chamber fills with smoke, giving the food its characteristic smokey flavor.

KAMADO

The egg-shaped kamado, a thick-walled ceramic cooker, is great for smoking foods at lower temperatures—usually between 150 and 250 degrees F—for long periods of time using only a small amount of charcoal. The size of the cooking space is limited, however; the largest models have a diameter of about 24 inches.

PIZZA OVEN

A wood-fired pizza oven reaches temperatures unattainable in an indoor oven—600 to 700 degrees F is common. It produces intense, even heat, resulting in pizzas with crisp crusts and sizzling toppings. Gas-powered versions with stone walls are available, but their hottest temperature is about 500 degrees F. Either of these ovens can also be used for baking bread, roasting vegetables, and cooking meat.

ADOBE OVEN

An adobe oven is a low-tech alternative to a pizza oven that will keep more cash in your wallet. The basic adobe oven is simply an enclosure made of hardened mud with a deep, arch-shaped opening in the front and a vent hole in the back.

CHURRASCO BARBECUE

Popular in Latin America, a churrasco barbecue cooks meat on a rotisserie using wood charcoal or firewood. It is different from a charcoal grill with a rotisserie because heat radiates from its oven-like walls, which helps seal in the juices and produce exceptionally tender cuts of cooked meat.

This roomy outdoor kitchen, left, has a large wood-fired oven with a terra-cotta roof to complement the built-in gas grill.

An electric smoker oven, opposite, has been built into a tiled outdoor cooking island.

Under-the-counter appliances not only look great but also afford cooks plenty of work space in this outdoor kitchen, above.

This gas grill's wok cooker, opposite, has a center trivet that converts to a burner grate to accommodate a large stock pot—perfect for lobster!

MORE OUTDOOR APPLIANCES

YOU'RE READY TO GRILL THE MEAT. What about the cheese, the condiments, and the drinks? It doesn't make sense to cook outdoors if you have to keep running back to the house for other items. Add a refrigerator and your outdoor cooking area becomes a working kitchen.

Under-counter refrigerators are the choice for most outdoor kitchens because they're out of sight, protected from the elements, and leave room for counter space. (A full-size standard refrigerator should only be considered in a large, sheltered kitchen in a temperate climate.) However, manu- facturers now make refrigerators for outdoor use. You will pay more money, but you'll get an appli- ance that has a large compressor to keep your food cold and includes wiring and electronics designed to withstand the elements. The best ones are made of stainess steel and stand up to the most extreme environments.

Most outdoor kitchen refrigerators start at $1,500; a 24-inch stainless-steel model could set you back more than $2,000. Make sure yours has heavy door hinges that create a good seal. It should be front-vented if you intend to install it under a countertop.

You could also check into a compact refrigera- tor drawer or a freezer drawer that you can fit under the counter.

ONE MORE THING...

TO REDUCE THE AMOUNT OF ENERGY your refrigerator uses, keep it out of direct sun- light and position it away from the grill or any other heat sources.

Other Appliance Amenities

IF YOU WANT YOUR OUTDOOR KITCHEN to be as efficient as its indoor counterpart, it makes sense to include some amenities. Small appliances are as indispensable outside as they are inside. As long as you keep them sheltered, you can equip your outdoor kitchen with a blender, coffeemaker, toaster oven, waffle maker, juicer, and whatever else you desire.

Warming Drawers. One popular amenity is a warming drawer with temperature controls to keep finished food items warm until dinner is ready. The variable-moisture control will help maintain the proper food texture, whether it's moist or crisp or somewhere in between. An ice maker also comes in handy. It will require a water line. Some models may also require a drain. If you're going to entertain often, look for a model that makes a large amount—25 to 35 pounds of ice—

in a short time. Compact ice maker-refrigerator combos are also available.

Wine Coolers. Nothing complements a fine meal better than a perfect glass of wine. A wine cooler with an adjustable thermostat stores your favorite vino at the perfect temperature. Many wine coolers include automatic settings for red or white wine, too. You can also store any cold beverage or chilled food, such as fruit, in a wine cooler.

A roomy warming drawer below the grill or cooktop is a handy addition when you are preparing an elaborate dinner for guests, opposite.

A beer tap or beverage dispenser, below, has become a popular addition to an outdoor kitchen. Portable models have castors that let you move the party to another area.

MORE KITCHEN COMPONENTS

MOST STORAGE PLANS for an outdoor kitchen begin with the grill, either by building the grill into a counter (an island or peninsula) or by flanking a freestanding grill with counters.

Outdoor-kitchen counters can be custom-built or assembled from prefabricated components. The former are permanent structures built of masonry, metal, or wood. If you want to take your outdoor kitchen with you when you move, consider prefabricated counters, which cost less than custom ones and do not require a building permit. For those reasons, these units are becoming increasingly popular.

The trellis and arbor blend with the wood custom cabinets and deck, here.

Custom Counters

Many outdoor kitchens are made of concrete, stone, or brick—and for good reason. Masonry materials are chosen for their appearance and durability. Note, however, that this durable structure must sit on a solid foundation. In many cases, this means a steel-reinforced concrete slab that is thick enough—typically 4 to 6 inches—to satisfy local building codes.

Concrete block is a rugged, structurally sound material that is less expensive and more readily available than stone. Rough-face concrete block has an attractive stone-like texture. Or you can cover block with a stone, brick, or stucco facing.

Masonry walls built with stone or brick are another option. Rustic stone blends naturally with the landscape and contrasts nicely with the stainless-steel accessories. Brick fits into almost every outdoor setting and complements nearly every architectural style. Most people prefer the look of common brick, but it's porous and less durable than firebrick, which is slightly larger, heavier, and more expensive.

Counters can also be *framed with steel* and covered with concrete backer board. These units are strong, withstand freezing temperatures, and, like those built of concrete block, are fire resistant. Steel framing is lighter than concrete block. So much lighter, in fact, that a well-framed deck can support it.

Don't discount a *wood-framed* counter. It's the easiest type to build, and it offers plenty of design flexibility. As long as the countertop is not made from concrete or another heavy material, your wood-framed counter will probably be light enough to rest on your deck. Wood's biggest downside is that it's flammable, requiring it to have an insulating jacket. Check the grill manufacturer's recommendations to be sure the wood surfaces will be protected from heat.

Teak cabinets and a stone countertop afford plenty of storage and work space for this outdoor kitchen, above.

This all-stone kitchen, left, complete with slate countertops, seems as if it was carved out of the landscape.

Facings and Finishes

HOW DOES IT LOOK? Will it hold up? Those are the key questions to ask when you're selecting material for your custom kitchen counters. Here are the most common choices:

Tile. If you'd like straight lines and a contemporary look, your best bet is tile facing. Stone tiles cut into straight-sided pieces provide a natural feel. Possibilities include granite, marble, and slate. Ceramic tile comes in a wide variety of colors, shapes, and textures.

Natural Stone. If you have stainless-steel doors and appliances, they will blend nicely with natural stone. Your outdoor kitchen will have a rugged, rustic look if you use random shapes and sizes for a jigsaw-puzzle appearance. For a refined look on top of the counter, choose slab granite.

Manufactured Stone. Also referred to as engineered stone or "faux stone," manufactured stone is a cheaper alternative to the real thing. The textures, shapes, and colors of real stone can be replicated with exacting detail these days. Manufactured stone is lighter than natural stone, too, so it's easier to install, and it stands up well to harsh weather.

Brick. To bring that cozy, traditional feel to the backyard, many people opt for a brick facing. Common brick, which blends well with many home styles, is popular, but other face bricks are also available.

Stucco. Stucco, a mixture of cement, sand, lime, and water churned into a thick paste, blends into a natural setting. Left natural, stucco facing has a soft, subdued appearnace. After it dries, it can be painted any color you wish.

Decorative stone tiles have been set in an attractive pattern here. They're a handsome counterpoint to the sleek, modern look of the stainless steel.

Prefabricated Grill Counters. Prefabricated counters are available in two ways. First is the completely ready-made unit that is available at major home-improvement centers. Second is a semicustom model, which is the way to go if you want more design input. With this option, you choose from an assortment of modular units to achieve a configuration to your liking. You can select from a variety of features, options, and exterior finishes. The most common finishes are tile, stone, brick, and stucco with either a concrete, stone, tile, or stainless-steel countertop. You provide cutout dimensions for the grill and other components. The manufacturer builds the counter, which is typically steel framed, off site, according to your specs, and delivers it in as little as two weeks. The process is easy and affordable, which makes this option attractive to most homeowners.

Customizing allows you to design an outdoor kitchen to your exact specifications.

Outdoor Sound and TV

OUTDOOR KITCHENS are incorporating the same amenities as their indoor counterparts. Manufacturers are making LCD and plasma televisions to weather the elements. Now you can sit down to a meal and bask in Mother Nature—without missing a moment of the big game or a movie. Outdoor TVs feature an all-weather enclosure that protects the components from rain, dirt, and scratches. They also come with an anti-glare, scratch-resistant front panel that enhances contrast to aid outdoor viewing. Even the cables and remote control are designed to be watertight.

Audio is also becoming an amenity people don't want to do without while they're outdoors. Many outdoor kitchens are outfitted with high-quality sound components—speakers, channel amplifiers, and CD/Mp3 players—that are corrosion resistant and waterproof. The models are often called "marine grade," because they were designed to be installed on boats and yachts.

Outdoor rooms may incorporate all the amenities and comforts of the main house—in this case, a flat-screen plasma TV and fireplace, above.

A custom-designed outdoor space, below, includes three separate areas for cooking, dining, and watching TV in the open air, day or night.

Bar Islands

When creating your ultimate outdoor kitchen, there is no need to limit yourself. Include a bar island in your plans. A bar can come in handy by providing a dedicated area for drinks, glasses, shakers, and jiggers, but it doesn't have to be large. Some built-in "beverage stations" are as small as 14 inches wide. Large or small, an outdoor bar should be functional. Including a stainless-steel sink makes it easier to mix drinks, and it can double as a prep and cleanup area. Storage compartments can hold lemons, limes, olives, and other key garnishes, which can be sliced with ease if your bar has a slide-away cutting board. A speed rail, which is a bottle-holding rack, allows you to easily organize and access wines.

Less-costly storage options are also available. A bar cart on casters can easily roll anywhere the action is. Many manufacturers offer these portable carts with a lot of the storage features a built-in bar includes.

Much cheaper still is a party cooler on a stand that can keep plenty of drinks cold up to 12 hours. And, of course, there is always the typical cooler that can go from the outdoor kitchen to the beach, the boat, and your kid's soccer game.

Deluxe bar islands can come equipped with storage drawers and cabinets, a beverage tap, a small refrigerator, and a cold-water sink.

CABINETS

SOME HOMEOWNERS choose true cabinets for their outdoor space. Full-size cabinets offer a more finished look, greater usable storage space, and are more accessible than their framed or masonry counterparts.

Wood cabinets tend to expand and contract outdoors, so keep them well sealed, and protect them under a roof, awning, or some other overhead structure. Because wood is combustible, maintain fire safety at all times, too.

Stainless-steel cabinets are another popular outdoor-cabinet option. They come complete with drawers and doors and can be installed next to your house, against masonry, or left freestanding in an island configuration. Stainless-steel cabinets are hygienic and easy to keep clean. They are also impervious to the elements—they won't deteriorate when they are exposed to ultraviolet rays. If you think that stainless steel looks cold, manufacturers now make these cabinets with a wood-tone look. You can have all the warmth of wood, without the maintenance.

Outdoor-cabinet makers offer units made from marine-grade, high-density polyethylene (HDPE), a product that is engineered for outdoors and designed to withstand the elements. These outdoor cabinets come in a variety of styles, with adjustable legs, and cost about 50 percent less than stainless steel. Unlike wood, no painting, staining, or sealing is required.

These sturdy outdoor cabinets, top left, can stand up to all kinds of weather while providing generous storage space.

Stainless-steel cabinetry, left, is a wise choice. It not only looks modern but is also weather-resistant and easy to clean.

Other Storage Ideas

IT'S ALWAYS NICE to have a little extra storage space, but it's not only about volume. Consider accessibility and organization, too. Having the proper storage will decrease clutter and increase efficiency.

Pullout shelves mounted under the sink or in a base cabinet are a must. A pullout shelf that slides on heavy-duty gliders keeps supplies handy—and you from having to bend over to reach objects in the back of a drawer. Another functional item is an under-sink organizer. It fits around the plumbing, making the most of the limited but valuable space you have. Simple, easy-to-install organizers on the inside of a door work wonders. Use plastic ones on your base cabinets to store canned goods and aluminum foil. For those spots that aren't convenient to reach, consider a lazy Susan. Get one to fill a corner cabinet—lazy Susans may be round, half round, D-shaped, and pie-shaped—and you'll make better use of that space that otherwise would have been hard to reach.

Last, but certainly not least, is the kitchen cart. All storage doesn't have to be built. If the space is tight, a kitchen cart can store dishes, utensils, towels, and almost anything else you may need. A cart can also double as an extra serving area, and you can use it as a portable bar.

> **» TIP** Put unused space to work by hanging pots and pans from a trellis. Do so and you'll reclaim valuable cabinet space. Hang them within easy reach, of course!

A simple drawer below the grill comes in handy for storing spices and utensils, top right.

A kitchen cart or a table with a shelf, right, can double as a buffet when you are ready to serve food.

CHAPTER 6

SHEDS

YOU CRAM STUFF IN THE CRAWL SPACE, BOX IT UP IN THE BASEMENT, AND STACK SO MUCH IN THE GARAGE THAT THERE'S NO ROOM FOR YOUR CAR. OKAY, IT'S TIME FOR A BACKYARD STORAGE SHED. A DEDICATED STORAGE SHED PROVIDES A PLACE FOR MOWERS, BIKES, LADDERS, TIRES, OLD FURNITURE, AND EVERYTHING ELSE CLOGGING UP YOUR GARAGE OR ATTIC. STORAGE SHEDS ARE ALSO A WEATHERPROOF HOME FOR TRACTORS, SNOW THROWERS, GARDEN TILLERS, AND YOUR COLLECTION OF TOOLS. THERE'S A GROWING TREND TOWARD LARGER SHEDS BEING EVERYTHING FROM POTTING SHEDS TO STUDIOS, AS WELL AS WORKSHOPS AND HOME OFFICES, TOO. MORE AND MORE, GUYS ARE USING SHEDS AS AN EXTRA ROOM RATHER THAN HAVING AN ADDITION PUT ON THEIR HOME. IN FACT, IT'S HARD TO CALL THESE STANDALONE SPACES SHEDS. SOME HAVE VAULTED CEILINGS, ARCHED FRONT DOORS, WINDOWS, SMALL PORCHES, LOFTS, HEATING, AIR CONDITIONING, AND PLUMBING. THE BOTTOM LINE? THERE IS A SHED OUT THERE THAT WILL MEET YOUR NEEDS, WHATEVER THEY ARE.

BUILDING YOUR DREAM SHED

Sheds these days come in many styles. This saltbox design looks more like an elegant cottage than a storage shed.

OUTDOOR STORAGE SHEDS are not merely utilitarian items. In addition to their functionality, their looks affect the overall appearance of the property. Many outdoor sheds come in attractive designs, allowing homeowners to hide their clutter with class and style. The shed you choose should complement your home. Select one with a rustic design with board-and-batten siding for a country-style house. If your house's style is more formal, choose a shed with features to match. If your house has an arched window, install the same type of window in your shed. Also think about integrating the shed into the surrounding landscape. Planting annual and perennial beds around the shed and installing a trellis or two near the walls will make the shed look as though it belongs on the property rather than sticking out like a sore thumb.

Building Codes and Permits

BEFORE BUILDING A SHED, bring a set of plans to your local building department and apply for a building permit. If you hire a contractor, he can take care of this step for you. In some towns, a building permit is required for sheds that are larger than 10 x 12 feet. Check with your building department. Building codes may determine how far sheds must be set back from property lines and what materials may be acceptable for siding. Local building codes also dictate the type of foundation needed. Requirements differ from town to town, but in most areas, sheds that are 10 x 10 feet or smaller can be built on concrete blocks set on the ground. Larger sheds must be supported by poured-concrete footings dug below the frost line. The building inspector may have to examine the trenches or pier holes before you pour the concrete.

If you're thinking about wiring the shed, you'll probably need an electrical permit. If your power needs are minimal—a stereo and a couple of lamps—you can probably connect a new circuit to your home's circuit-breaker box, run a wire to the shed, and add some wall outlets. If you require more power, you may need a new panel box or an upgrade to your home's electrical system. It's a good idea to check with your homeowners' association, if you have one, before buying a shed. The building may have to be situated so that it's not visible from the street, or its roof may have to match that of the main house.

A common garden shed is painted creatively to stand out in the landscape.

Location and Style

Siting the shed is another important consideration too many homeowners overlook. To get the most use of your shed, keep it close to the driveway or house. Kids are more likely to put away their bikes and sports equipment if the shed is near. Never build a shed at the bottom of a hill where water collects. Also have at least three feet of open space around all sides to make room for repairs and allow for air to circulate freely.

Choosing the style is important, too. Sheds with gable roofs offer tall walls that are useful for putting up shelves and hanging long-handled tools. But they provide little headroom when you stand near the walls. Gambrel-style roofs, or barn roofs, have shorter walls but much more head-room. If you like the look of a gambrel roof but need wall storage, order a shed with 7- or 8-foot-tall sidewalls. That way, you get ample wall storage and extra headroom.

Logs made from trees that were cut down on the site were used for this custom-built shed. Double doors allow the homeowner to move equipment in and out easily.

ONE MORE THING ...

Door Placement

IF YOU'RE PLANNING to make your shed 10 x 20 feet or larger, place the doors in the middle of the sidewall. Doors located in the end gable will make it hard to reach items stored at the very back of the shed.

UPSCALE MODELS

IF YOU DON'T NEED THE SHED for your snowblower as much as you do for extra living space, there are any number of options available. Today you can have a plush shed or backyard building that functions more as a room—an exercise or hobby studio, pool house, home office, even a guest cottage. It can come with double casement windows, interior cedar ceilings, and a front door similar to that of your home's. Some manufacturers offer home office kits that are made specifically for the backyard. One kit offers a 10 × 12-foot finished office with an attached 9 × 9-foot deck. It comes in panels, including floors, walls with prehung windows and doors, and a shingled roof.

The most-popular sizes of backyard buildings are 10 × 12 and 8 × 15 feet because, in most places, one or the other is the largest size you can build without a permit. Any bigger and you'll have to spend $700 to $1,500 for permits or a city fee.

With a few added touches, you can transform a shed into a getaway for you and your family. Open up the space with upscale options such as French doors and large windows. Skylights that crank open add dramatic daylight and vent hot air. Layer on the comfort with a daybed to create a spot for reading or napping. Set up a bistro table and chairs for morning coffee, watching the game, or a juice-box cooldown for the kids. Hang curtains on the windows for a little privacy, and roll out a plush rug for warmth in winter.

A vinyl-sided shed can be dressed up with charming details such as a cupola, shutters, and inserts in the double doors.

Extras

UPGRADE OPTIONS ABOUND. Buyers can choose thicker rigid-foam insulation in the ceiling (an inch and a half is standard). Insulated clear-glass panels can replace thin polycarbonate. Sustainable bamboo flooring is a choice over the standard oriented strand board. There's even a small heat pump that can be installed to warm the shed in winter and cool it in summer.

Many people like their "luxe" sheds to fit in with the decor of the house. Paint your shed and its trim to match, and coordinate the roof shingles as well. Some manufacturers make cedar-shake roofing specifically for sheds.

Dress up the shed even more by adding a cupola or weathervane. For the perfect finishing touch, repeat the landscaping pattern outside your front door in the area around your shed. Include decorative stones, garden benches or chairs, pergolas, lanterns, or bird feeders.

A custom-built wood shed is easy on the eye with its arched roof and provides plenty of functional storage space on the walls and doors.

SHED-BUILDING FACTS

WHETHER IT'S A STORAGE SHED or a backyard building, it will be metal, resin (plastic), vinyl-sided, or all wood. There are pros and cons regarding all four of these materials.

Metal sheds are made from galvanized steel, aluminium, or corrugated iron. They are a good choice for long-term strength. In addition, they are resistant to fire, rot, and termites. Aluminum is the metal of preference because it won't rust. Steel, on the other hand, is less durable because it is prone to corrosion.

These days metal storage sheds come with a baked-enamel coating to make them more visually appealing and durable. It's not difficult to dent some metal sheds. In addition, heavy accumulation of snow and ice can damage the roof of a metal shed. If a metal shed is your first choice, you've got to protect it from heavy winds by attaching it to a concrete foundation with screws.

ONE MORE THING...

IF YOU LIVE IN AN AREA that gets a fair amount of snow and you're thinking of purchasing a metal shed, be sure to buy one that offers a roof-reinforcement kit. It costs $50 to $100, depending on the shed size, but can boost the load capacity of the roof by 50 percent.

A gambrel-roof shed provides lots of wall and overhead space for storage and double doors for easy access.

Resin, or plastic, sheds are made of heavy molded plastics such as PVC and polyethylene and are less expensive than metal sheds. The plastic is not susceptible to termite and insect damage and is virtually maintenance free. The double-panel walls resist dents and dings. Some higher-quality sheds are UV-resistant and include powder-coated metal components that give the shed rigidity. Many plastic sheds are modular, allowing you to easily add extensions, shelves, lofts, windows, skylights, and other accessories.

Vinyl-sided sheds are typically built with standard wood-framing construction and oriented strand board (OSB) on the walls covered with standard vinyl siding. Vinyl-sided sheds never need to be painted, are generally stronger than plastic or metal sheds, and are usually built to conform with the local building codes. They cost more than wood, metal, or plastic sheds.

Wood sheds have a natural look that can blend in well with garden environments. Depending on the style and color you choose, wood sheds can either be made to stand out as an outdoor building in the garden or blended into its surroundings. Despite the strength of wood, it can rot, split, warp, or become susceptible to mold and mildew over time. Stains and preservative products can be applied to wood sheds to prevent damage caused by exposure to rain, UV light, harsh climatic conditions, fungal attack, and wood-boring insects. Some types of wood, such as cedar, are more naturally resistant to water damage.

A wood-sided shed ages beautifully through the seasons. The dark roof shingles are a stunning counterpoint to the white and pink garden that borders it.

Build It From Scratch—Or Not

THERE ARE THREE BASIC WAYS to get a wood shed: order a set of plans and build it from scratch; buy a ready-to-assemble kit and build it yourself; or hire a contractor who specializes in building sheds.

Building a shed from plans is your least-expensive option. Of course it entails the most work and time and requires moderate to advanced carpentry skills. Mail-order shed plans typically cost $20 to $30 and are available from companies that sell home plans. Local shed contractors are another source of plans.

If you're not up to building a shed from scratch, consider a *ready-to-assemble shed*. A kit is an appealing compromise between economy and ease. The large preassembled panels go together like a jigsaw puzzle. All the parts are precut, so there's nothing to saw—even the doors are prehung. In most cases, you can put up a shed in a single day. Prices start at around $320.

Build-your-own shed kits can be purchased in a variety of styles, sizes, and materials. You can choose a quaint little cottage-style wooden shed, vinyl kits that look like small barns, or metal kits. Another advantage is that shed kits include the trim and accessories you need without having to purchase them later.

The easiest way to get a *custom* storage shed that is tailored to meet your exact needs is to hire a local contractor. This is also the most-expensive option—figure on $2,000 to $3,000 for a 10 x 10-foot shed. But this option does provide the greatest flexibility because most contractors will alter a style or custom-build a shed to suit your site, storage requirements, and personal taste. What's more, once the foundation is set, the contractor can usually build the entire shed in one day by preassembling some of the components in the workshop beforehand.

Keep in mind that not all wood sheds are created equal. Those made of untreated pine or fir typically show signs of rot or insect infestation within two years. Look for a shed made of decay-resistant lumber, cedar, or redwood. In addition, the floor frame and support posts should be pressure-treated wood rated for ground contact, which offers optimum protection from rot and wood-boring bugs. Pay particular attention to hardware and fasteners, screws, nails, and bolts. Use metal parts that are either hot-dipped galvanized metal or stainless steel.

Shed-kit designs can even include a front porch and railings, far left.

You can paint any shed to match the colors of the main house, left.

CHAPTER 6: SHEDS

Preparing the Shed Site

A common misconception is that a shed should be elevated on cinder blocks to help prevent rot and insect damage. This may have been the case 30 years ago, but since the introduction of pressure-treated lumber and today's more durable sidings, this is no longer necessary.

A crushed-stone base, four to six inches deep, is one of the best ways to prepare the site. Be sure to use *crushed* stone—½-inch is a good diameter—as opposed to pea stone. When you are preparing the site, extend the size of the base, making it 2 feet longer and wider than the actual size of the shed. This will prevent mud caused by roof runoff from splashing against the siding.

Some towns recommend concrete piers, usually 10 inches in diameter. You should contact the shed builder or retailer for recommended placement. A cement slab is one of the more-expensive ways to prepare a shed site, but has its benefits. A slab will keep the shed level and prevents grass and weeds from growing both under and around the structure. Most companies will place the shed on concrete blocks or patio blocks in order to level it. But concrete blocks have a tendency to settle into the ground over time, which will cause the shed to fall out of level and hinder the use of the shed doors. If you choose to use patio blocks, it's a good idea to dig a trench that is 1 foot wide and 4 to 6 inches deep around the perimeter of the shed, and then fill it with some type of stone or gravel. This will prevent runoff from splashing dirt on the siding and also keep grass and weeds from growing against it.

Some homeowners may simply decide to place the structure directly on the ground. Depending on the shed's construction, this should be fine. Be sure that there is a pressure-treated floor system and base. It is also important to run pressure-treated timbers underneath and perpendicular to the floor joists in order to elevate the shed and allow adequate ventilation.

A concrete-pier foundation provides stability for a shed when the ground freezes and thaws, left.

This lakeside shed, opposite, is built with enough room for all of kinds of fishing gear.

ONE MORE THING...

IF YOU LIVE IN AN AREA that experiences high winds, take precautions to anchor your shed. You can install straps on the inside, securing the roof to the walls and the walls to the base. Secure the base with ground augur anchors.

Roof Styles. The three most popular types of shed roofs are, gable, gambrel, and saltbox.

A *gable roof* is in the shape of an inverted V with two triangular ends. A *gambrel roof,* which is very common on sheds, combines two gable roofs of differing slopes. The lower slope on each side is steep, which provides more usable space in the upper area or headroom. A *saltbox roof* has a long, rear slope. Headroom and overhead storage is limited to the front of the structure, but with wide doors, this can be a practical choice if you have limited space for a shed.

Siding. *Rough-sawn pine* is rustic in appearance and relatively inexpensive. It is commonly used for board-and-batten construction. Rough-sawn pine requires more maintenance than most siding types and typically needs to be repainted or stained every few years. Even with the drawbacks, rough-sawn pine is a popular choice. Be sure to ask if the pine is kiln dried, otherwise it could shrink and warp.

Vinyl siding is a great choice for homeowners who are not fond of maintenance. It is also a good choice for those who would like the shed to match

their vinyl-sided homes in appearance. Although vinyl siding is, for the most part, impervious to weathering, it is not for everyone. Unlike on wooden sheds, a simple mar in the siding cannot be touched up with paint. The material is also susceptible to dents and dings. If you crack a corner with a line trimmer or dent the siding with an errant baseball throw, the repairs can be more costly than they would be if the shed is wood.

Cedar has been a popular siding for wood sheds. Although most sheds are sided with red cedar some manufacturers utilize the less-expensive white cedar. Red cedar must be primed well before painting, and in some cases the knots will still bleed through the paint. When choosing red cedar, be sure that it is not constructed with "cut-offs" or "shorts." These are small pieces of wood that can make boards look almost like puzzle pieces put together. They might reduce the cost, but they can also make a shed substantially weaker than one built with standard lengths of wood.

There is also a *plywood* siding with a ⅛-inch Douglas fir wood-composite face. It looks natural, resists dents, checks, and cracks, and is 100 percent clear, meaning it has no wood or synthetic patches. This product also holds paint exceptionally well, tends to be less costly than red cedar and vinyl, and requires very little maintenance.

This roomy shed, opposite, has been designed as a guest room. The metal roof will shed snow in winter.

A log-style shed, top right, complete with window boxes, is custom-built to fit into its natural setting.

get smart

«It's in the Details
A vent that allows stale air out and fresh air inside the shed is a good idea, especially if you use the structure as a workspace or for storing paint and other chemicals.

»» TIP Any electrical outlet you add outdoors must be GFCI protected and approved for this use.

CHAPTER 6: SHEDS

Customize Your Shed

UPGRADING WITH THE FOLLOWING ACCESSORIES will make your shed more functional and attractive to the eye.

• **Ramps.** A sturdy set of ramps is a must for moving wheeled power equipment or hand trucks into or out of your shed.

• **Windows and Skylights.** Natural light increases visibility and makes the space more user friendly. In most cases, you can even order shutters and window boxes to accompany your windows and further enhance the aesthetics of your shed.

• **Loft.** Increase the usable space in your shed with a loft. The loft is designed to allow you to park the mower underneath and still give you a solid storage platform overhead.

• **Extra-Wide Doors.** Sheds with extra-wide doors are useful if you plan to store bulky items such as lawn mowers, motor-cycles, or similarly large items. Make sure the entry door is wide enough to accommodate your largest piece of equip-ment. Many outdoor sheds that are at least 8 x 10 feet come with double doors, which usually eliminate the concern.

• **Shelves.** Organize your tools and materials on handy shelves designed by the manufacturer specifically for your shed. There are several types of sheds that include grooves in the walls to easily insert shelves.

• **Workbench.** If you plan to use the barn as a gardening or hobby shop, a good workbench is a must.

Window boxes add natural charm, top right.

Windows light up a garden potting shed, right.

Shelves add extra storage to this garden shed, opposite.

CHAPTER 7

BEDROOMS, BATHROOMS & STORAGE

TODAY, A BEDROOM CAN BE MORE THAN JUST A PLACE TO SLEEP. A LOT OF PEOPLE SEE IT AS A PERSONAL GETAWAY FROM THE PRESSURES OF DAILY LIVING. AS SUCH, IT SHOULD HAVE CERTAIN AMENITIES FOR REAL COMFORT—RESTFUL FURNISHINGS, GREAT STORAGE THAT MIGHT INCLUDE A WALK-IN CLOSET, AND A SPA-LIKE BATH WHERE YOU CAN SOOTHE SORE MUSCLES FROM A TOUGH MATCH ON THE TENNIS COURT OR A STRESSFUL DAY AT WORK. A WELL-PLANNED SPACE MIGHT ALSO INCLUDE VIDEO OR A HIGH-END SOUND SYSTEM, A GAS FIREPLACE WITH A REMOTE CONTROL, AND ACCESS TO AN OUTDOOR DECK OR PATIO. EVEN A SIMPLE BEDROOM CAN BE CONVERTED TO CATER TO YOU ALONE. HERE ARE SOME IDEAS FOR CREATING GREAT PERSONAL SPACES—BOTH BASIC AND SUBLIME.

A WAY WITH COLOR

White trim and bedding look crisp against a background of blue walls. This classic scheme is always a good choice in a bedroom.

IF YOU NEED A STARTING PLACE, begin with color. Don't be afraid of it. A fresh coat of paint can completely transform a room, updating it with trendy colors and changing the mood of the space. For example, rich earthy hues will make the room feel snug and warm while fresh green and, especially, blue have a cooling effect. In general, restful colors are best; anything bright is too invigorating for a room where you need to relax. If you use a deeply saturated color on the wall, add pure white or another light neutral in bed linens or window treatments to give the eye a rest.

If you have reservations about using color, try it on an accent wall—the wall behind the bed, for example. Complement this wall by painting a softer tone of the same color on the other walls, or keep them neutral by using an off-white paint. If you want to play it very safe, buy only a quart of paint and test the color. Try it in different places around the room, and look at it at various times of the day in both natural and artificial light.

Don't forget the ceiling. After all, it is the first thing you'll see when you open your eyes in the morning. For a fresh approach, paint it a pale sky blue. It will make the room feel just a bit larger and airy. Finish the look with crown molding.

Versatile wood shutters offer the best control over light and air, while adding a strong architectural feature to this room's sitting area.

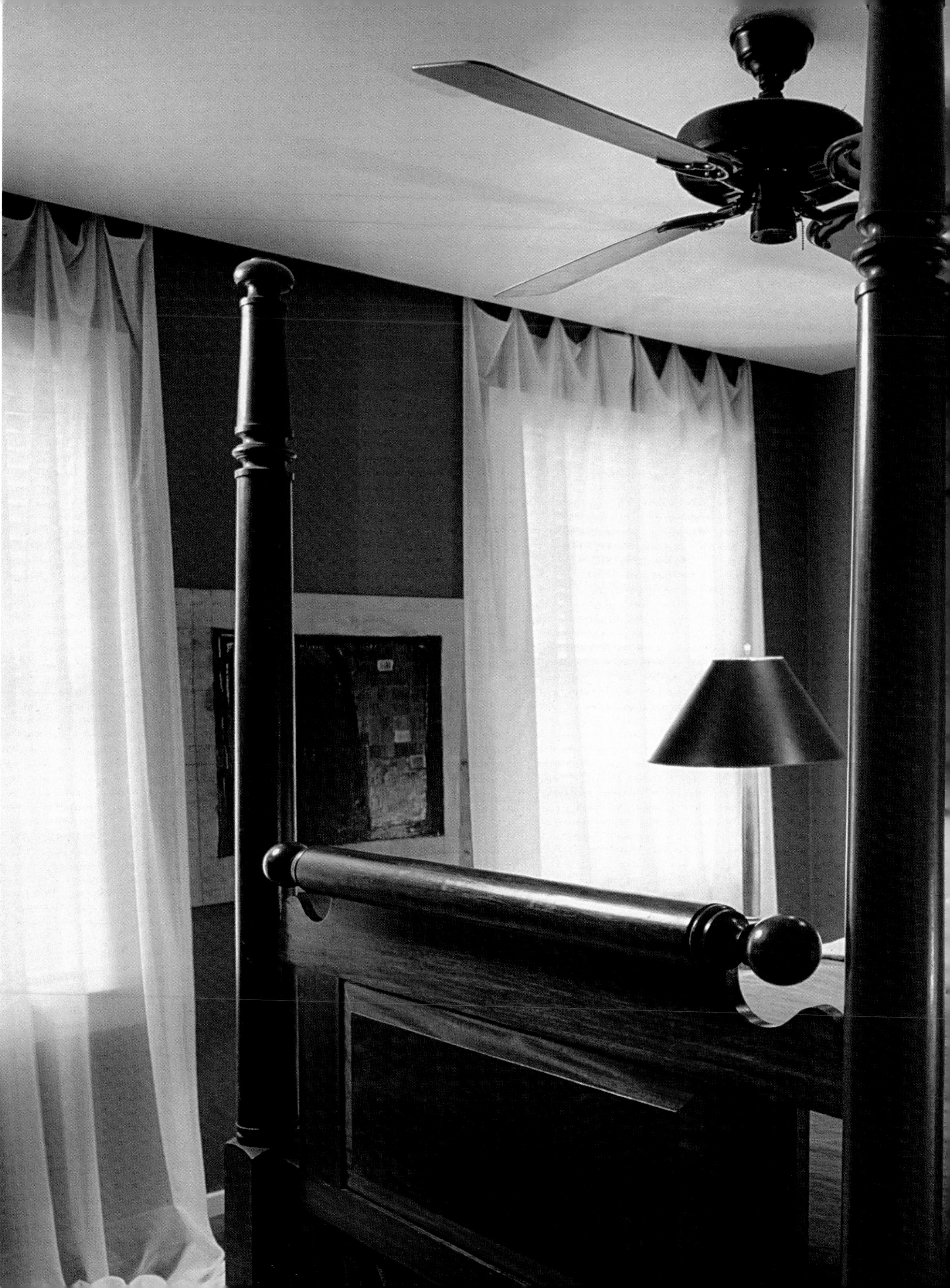

A LIGHT TOUCH

LIGHTING, BOTH NATURAL AND ARTIFICIAL, is important in creating atmosphere. If the room receives lots of sunlight, you should find stylish ways to control it. Window treatments are key. Covering the bedroom window in layers is a good idea. This way you have the option of full light, filtered or partial light, or total blackout for sleeping in on lazy mornings.

Shades, blinds, or shutters allow you to control the amount of natural light that enters the room without entirely blocking fresh air when you want it. Heavily lined curtains or shades will keep out the morning sun and provide insulation against the cold during the winter.

Most types of window treatments are available in standard sizes to fit stock windows if you don't want to go the custom route. You can find them in department stores or home centers.

Cellular Shades. Made of spun polyester, honeycomb shades are extremely flexible, making them a good choice to fit windows of unusual shapes as well as standard units. They come in single, double, or triple combs. The combs give this product its distinctive look, but they also trap air, making these shades good thermal and sound insulators. Lightweight, honeycombs can be installed vertically or, more conventionally, horizontally. They also offer varying levels of light control. On windows facing west, you might want to totally block out all light on hot days; if your bedroom faces east, you may be more interested in keeping early-morning sun out of your eyes. On other windows, sheer or translucent shades may be more appropriate.

Floor-to-ceiling curtains soften morning sunshine while recessed lighting and a lamp provide good supplemental illumination.

Horizontal Blinds. While these blinds may be a chore to keep clean, their adjustable louvers offer great control. The more slats per foot, the less light will leak through the blind. And blinds with cord holes at the back of the slats close more tightly—a feature to look for if you want them to be light-tight. As for cleaning, some newer products have a factory-applied antistatic-electricity treatment to deter dust.

Wood and faux-wood horizontal blinds, which cost more than their metal and vinyl counterparts, are especially popular today. They are equally at home in rustic-style bedrooms and modern spaces. Wood blinds installed in high-humidity rooms should be warp- and mildew-resistant.

Window Shadings. Shadings feature opaque louvers sandwiched between sheer fabric panels. This lets in light while keeping glare to a minimum. Shadings are useful for sunny windows that face south or east. Once the shade is fully lowered, the horizontal slats can be opened, tilted for filtered light and partial view, or shut for complete privacy with the cord.

Horizontal blinds can be adjusted to control light, air flow, and privacy. In this combination guest room and office, closed blinds keep glare off the work surface while protecting the upholstery from sun damage.

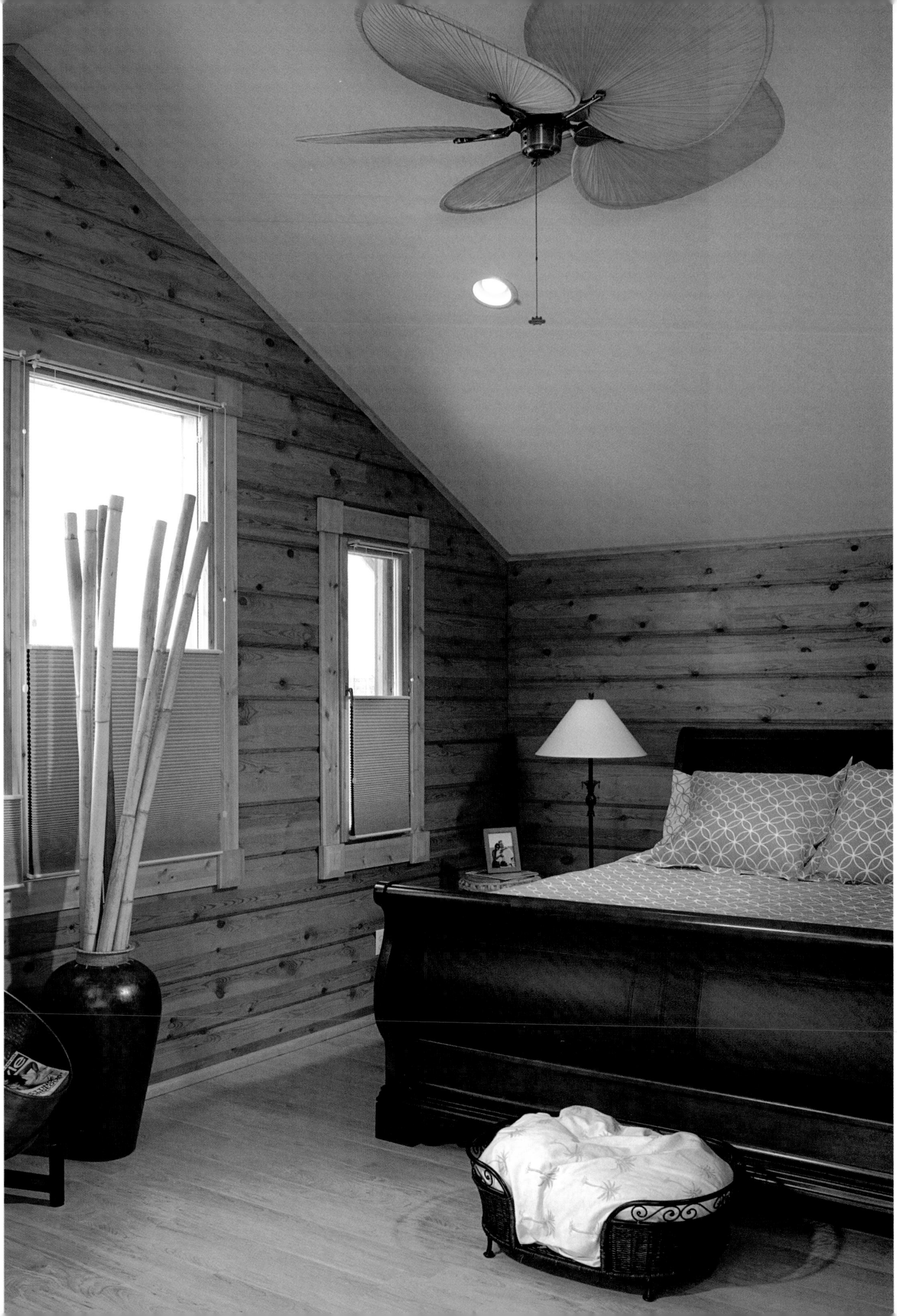

Roller Shades. Roller shades were once the standard for no-frills window coverings. Although they're available in translucent films and fabrics as well as traditional opaque materials, they aren't the best choice when it comes to light control—the shade is either up or down, offering no diffusion or direction. Installation options now include a reverse roll, where the shade material falls over the top of the roller, concealing it and resulting in a cleaner look. Roller shades give rooms a homey, retro feeling.

Vertical Blinds. Most commonly used over sliding-glass doors, vertical blinds are also at home with tall casement windows, fixed-glass windows, or bow windows, as well as with arch-top and angular windows. Vertical blinds have a contemporary look and can add a sense of drama with their strong lines. They also enhance the height of a room—something to keep in mind if ceilings are low in your bedroom. In vinyl, fabric, metal, or even matched to wallpaper (by slipping strips of the material into its front face), vertical blinds allow good air circulation when they are open and are an outstanding choice when it comes to protection from ultraviolet rays.

Shutters. With their distinctive appearance, shutters inject a lot of character into a room and the most versatility. The width of the slats has a lot to do with that. Vanes can measure up to 5½ inches (these are called "plantation shutters") and down to ¾ of an inch. Stained or painted solid-wood versions are traditional choices.

Bottom-mounted shades provide privacy without shutting out the view in this rustic-looking bedroom, opposite. A distinctive overhead fan keeps the room from getting stuffy.

ONE MORE THING...

Measuring Windows

DECIDE WHERE TO INSTALL the window treatment—inside or outside the window opening. An inside mount (typically for shades, blinds, and shutters) shows off a window's casing and its shape. An outside mount (typically for curtains) can disguise windows of unequal size.

Use a retractable metal measuring tape. For an *inside mount,* measure the length from the top of the frame to the sill, and then the inside width of the window. For an *outside mount,* decide where you want the rod and measure the width from bracket to bracket, adding at least 3 inches for a center overlap (if you're installing curtains).

Pleated shades, mounted inside the window opening here, have a tailored look.

Light Fixtures

Recessed lights or a ceiling fixture are suitable for general illumination, but don't forget about lamps for reading or watching TV. Wall sconces can add soft illumination that's fine for viewing or relaxing, but task lighting is necessary for reading a book. Be careful with overhead spotlights that are aimed straight down on a book or paper. Although they leave nightstands free for books, glasses, a clock radio, and what-not, they cast a shadow and can cause glare. A better option is a table lamp next to the bed, preferably one with an opaque or dark shade or a lamp that's attached to the end of the headboard or the wall next to the bed. Light should be even with your shoulder when you are sitting up in a reading position.

A dark lamp shade is a good idea when you want to keep the mood low key. It diffuses light and casts it only on the areas above and below the fixture.

ONE MORE THING ...

Light Tip

WHEN USING A TABLE LAMP, make sure to buy the right size shade. You should be able to see the lower edge of the shade—not the bulb—when you are seated. If this edge is below your eye level, you are not getting enough illumination from the source. The average seating eye level is 38 to 42 inches.

Spotlights directed toward the room's built-in cabinets, opposite, highlight their finish. The articulated table lamps are for reading.

BASIC BED AND HEADBOARD STYLES

THE STYLE OF THE BED you choose can quickly change the look of the room. If you're interested in something more than a box spring and mattress, look for a stylish headboard. There are all kinds of styles in a variety of wood tones. Metal is another option, and you can find anything, including polished brass, antique bronze, satin nickel and chrome, or wrought iron. For something unique, retrofit an old mantel, wood-paneled door, or ironwork found at a salvage yard. Or upholster a piece of plywood with leather or fabric that matches the window treatment.

In other words, the bed is probably going to be the largest piece of furniture in the room, so there are other ideas for one that are less conventional.

Trundle Bed. Instead of a box spring supporting a mattress, a trundle bed is a mattress that is supported by a frame. A second bed that is stored underneath can rolled out when you need it. Some come with a pop-up mechanism. Trundle beds are a great space-saving idea.

Platform Bed. This is a mattress resting on a wooden platform that provides support for the sleeper. The platform can include various drawers, cupboards, and cabinets for clothing, linen, and accessory storage. The headboard may be flanked with bookcases and built-in night tables. Platform beds are perfect when storage is at a premium.

Murphy Bed. Named for its designer, the Murphy bed folds up into an armoire, a wall unit, or even a closet when it's not in use. If you're short on space, or if the room has to double for living space or a home office, this is a great idea.

An upholstered headboard and throw pillows coordinate with the color of the walls here.

STORAGE

YOU CAN NEVER HAVE TOO MUCH storage space. Closet systems, either designed from scratch and built by a closet-organization company or purchased in a store ready to assemble, can double the capacity of an ordinary space by maximizing it.

The days when a bedroom closet could be out-fitted with a single metal pole are gone. Closets have to work harder now to accommodate contemporary storage needs. The best way to make your closet more efficient is to segment the space with a variety of shelves, cubbyholes, and clothes rods installed at different heights. This eliminates the wasted 3 or 4 feet below a dangling shirt and makes it easier to see an entire wardrobe at a glance.

Bedrooms can't have enough storage. A custom-designed built-in armoire, right, provides drawer and cabinet storage that is tailored to the owner's needs.

A walk-in closet and dressing room, opposite, offer organized storage and display space.

Arranging a Closet

TO ORGANIZE YOUR CLOSET, begin by sorting through your wardrobe, grouping like items of clothing so that you can see exactly what you have. At 64 inches, overcoats and bathrobes use up the most space when they hang from a rod. Next come trousers hung by the cuff, at 48 to 56 inches, followed by shirts, jackets, blazers, and folded pants that at 38 to 42 inches require the least space.

In addition to arranging things by size and type, you can organize items by how often you use them. Put everyday work clothes in the middle where you can easily see them, and then use the closet corners for out-of-season or less-used items, such as raincoats. And don't forget the back of the closet door where you can install a set of wall-mounted baskets for scarves or socks.

Dividers, shelves, and modular units are available in a wide range of prices and finishes. Filling a standard 8-foot-wide wall closet with professionally designed and installed shelving might cost as little as $500 for laminate. Upgrade to wood veneers or solid-hardwood shelving and you could pay $5,000. For the true clotheshorse, there are hydraulically operated rods that can be installed at the top of the closet. Pull them down when you need to reach something.

You can also invest in an armoire. Available in a range of styles and sizes, armoires usually have drawers for stowing sweaters and blankets, plus clothing rods for hanging shirts, jackets, and trousers. Add storage by buying nightstands with deep drawers and an upholstered ottoman with concealed storage beneath the seat.

Don't forget the area under the bed. Buy storage boxes, especially ones designed to fit under the box spring. Some are on wheels or glide on a track. These are great for seasonal items. You can also buy a folding screen. It not only makes for a neat room divider in the bedroom but can also hide clutter. Keep items without a permanent home in baskets and out of view.

Ready-to-assemble storage, right, can be configured to hold a host of items—from shoes and shirts to board games.

An open-plan living area, opposite, can still include lots of creative storage—even the space under a platform bed.

Ideas for Improving Any Closet

TAKE ADVANTAGE of all available space—bins on high shelves, rollout boxes on the floor in the back of the closet, even a third closet pole if your ceiling is over 9 feet high. These are all ideal for storing items you don't use all the time.

Natural light from skylights or windows is a plus, but beware of the fading that sunlight can produce. Windows also eat up space. If you use artificial light, be sure it is between you and the contents of the closet; if it's behind you, you'll cast a shadow on what you're trying to see. Incandescent bulbs can be a fire hazard in the tight, enclosed confines of a small closet. Fluorescent lighting is often the only code-compliant solution.

Arrange the most-used items around eye level, less-used below it, and least-used high above it. Most closets have too much hanging storage and far too little shelf or drawer storage.

To see all of your individual socks, ties, and underwear, use see-through wire bins, acrylic- or glass-fronted drawers, drawer dividers, and belt and tie racks. This will keep these items organized and visible.

Closets need some airflow and dehumidification or they become a breeding ground for mold, mildew, or insects. A bathroom-size fan, timed to go on and off at regular intervals, can circulate stale air and a small dehumidifier will keep things from getting musty.

Cedar closets can cause the whole bedroom to smell like a gerbil cage, so locate them in an attic or basement.

Natural light and under-shelf illumination add a lot to this dressing-room closet.

MORE ABOUT FURNISHINGS

ANY BEDROOM benefits from a focal point, a single element that immediately draws attention and anchors the room with it's visual weight or uniqueness. In the bedroom, the bed often plays this role. An important architectural feature, such as a fireplace, can be a focal point, as well.

Other furniture in the room can serve as a secondary focal point. It could be an antique blanket chest where you store your workout clothes at the foot of the bed or a large table used as a desk. Or it could be an oversize TV hanging on the wall opposite your bed.

When choosing storage furniture, called "case goods," think in terms of proportion, selecting a piece that balances the weight of the bed. As a general rule, allow at least 36 to 40 inches in front of chests and dressers to pull out drawers. Choose chairs, trunks, and tables in keeping with the scale of other pieces. Match the height of bedside tables to the bed, making sure the tables are at least as high as the top of the mattress. This will provide the best position for reading lamps that sit on the nightstands. Tuck a small bench at the foot of the bed or a small chair in one corner to add seating and an extra spot for books, magazines, clothes, blankets, or throws.

The unusual style of this platform bed, above right, attracts the eye while a similarly styled chair and ottoman offer plenty of comfort.

A large cabinet, right, visually separates the bedroom from the rest of the space in this open-plan design. It also provides storage.

Cracking the Codes

BEFORE YOU LOCATE A BEDROOM in a different part of the house—a newly finished basement or garage, for example—familiarize yourself with important building and safety codes. Here's what to keep in mind while you're making your plans.

For safe exits in event of fire, all sleeping rooms above or below grade are required to have either a door to the outside or a window with 5.7 square feet of operable area through which a person can escape.

Installation of a smoke detector in a sleeping room is required. Ironically, carbon monoxide detectors are not required by code in all places.

Flooring

If you hop out of bed barefoot, it is always comforting to have a well-padded carpet underfoot. On the other hand, the earthiness of wood or a look-alike laminate floor might be more appealing to you. You can soften and warm up these types of floors with area rugs. Carpet alternatives for anyone who has allergies can include vinyl, cork, ceramic tile, or stone, in addition to wood or a laminate.

Plush wall-to-wall carpeting adds coziness to this large bedroom, opposite.

Laminate flooring, right, creates a neutral palette for colorful furnishings.

An area rug, below, defines space and keeps the warm wood floor on view.

Allergy-Free Bedrooms

IN SPRING AND SUMMER, close the windows in the bedroom to keep out allergens. Depending on the temperature, you can use a ceiling fan or air conditioner to keep cool.

If you have plants in your bedroom, it's important to place a barrier between them and the carpet to prevent a problem with mold or mildew due to water spillage.

Painted walls are best for the bedroom because they are easy to clean. With wallpaper, you could have an allergic reaction to the paste.

When selecting a lamp for the bedroom, stay away from ornate designs because they can attract dust more easily than a simple design. Be sure to regularly clean and dust the lamp shades. Vacuum the curtains and rugs.

Hard floors—wood or stone—won't retain allergens the way rugs do. You should use carpeting only if you vacuum frequently—*at least* once a week.

Minimize the number of toss pillows on the bed. They collect a lot of dust and allergens. Ban your pet from the bed and, if you can manage it, the bedroom itself.

Use wooden shutters or blinds on bedroom windows. Curtains and fabric shades harbor allergens and are sometimes more difficult to clean.

Change and wash bed linens every week.

This roomy design shares a stone fireplace and the latest in home-theater equipment. The tile floors are easy to clean, which is important if you're prone to allergies.

BATHROOMS

The bathroom is where you start and end your day. It's also a place to relax and recharge, complete with steam shower and spa tub. Bath time can be an experience for the senses with the option of built-in audio systems, chromatherapy (using mood-enhancing colors), and even tubside refrigeration for cold beverages or to store organic skin products and medications that need to be kept cold. Bigger may be better, but you can equip any size bath with items designed to pamper you.

This cabin-inspired design transforms a utilitarian space into something special.

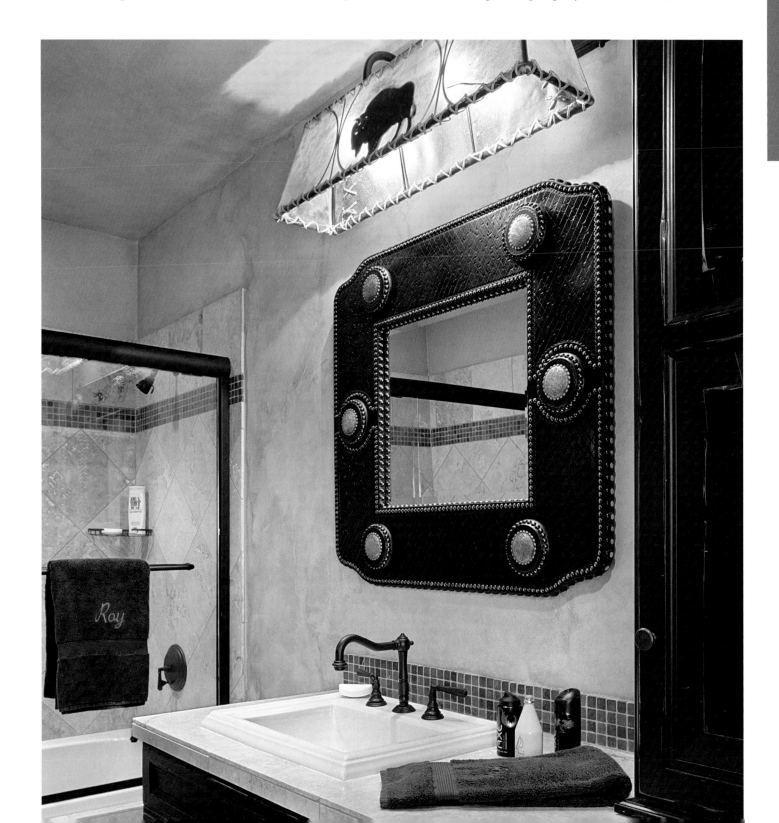

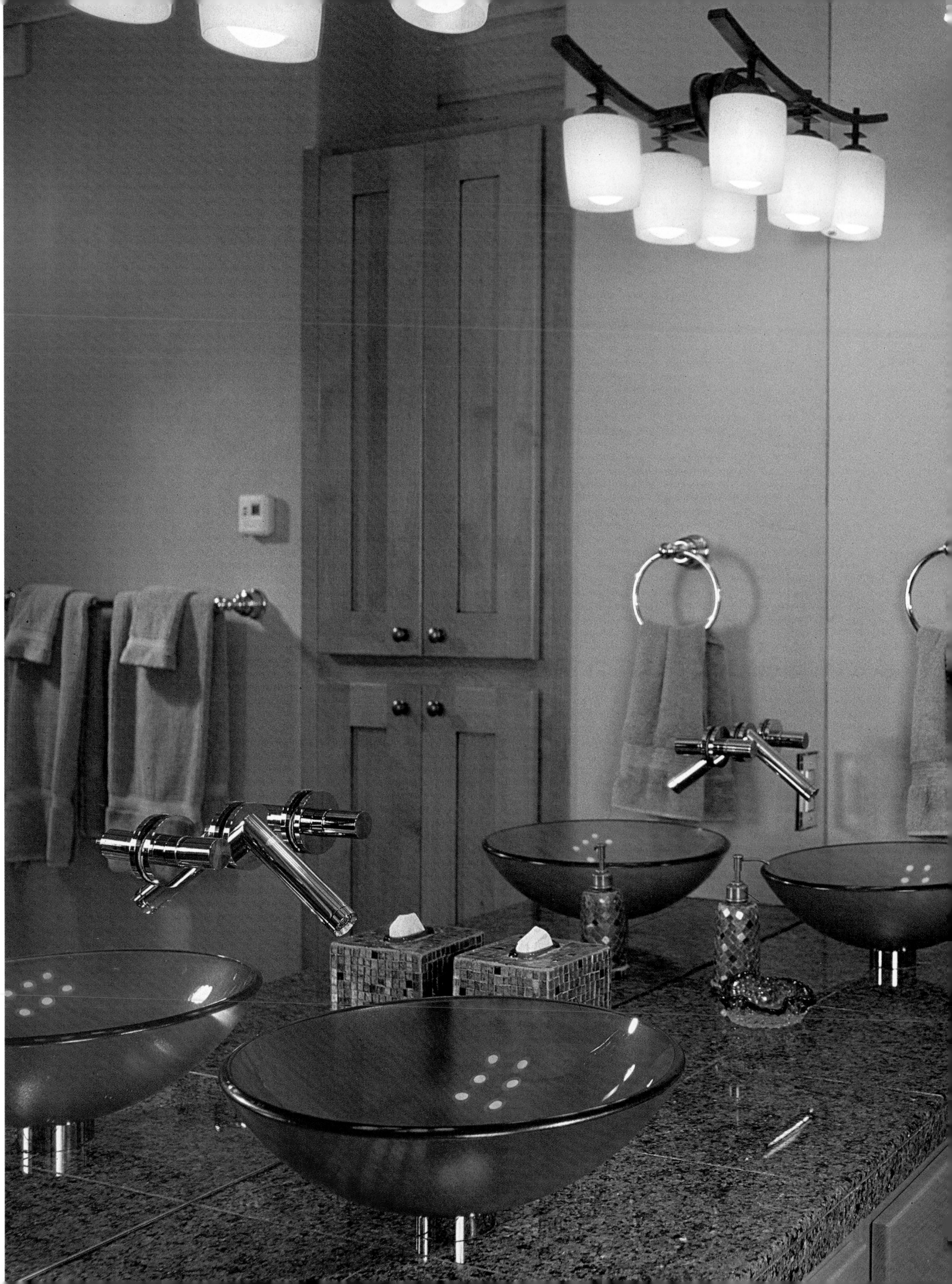

Surfacing Options

Ceramic tile has always been the material of choice in a bathroom because it is impervious to water and offers so many design possibilities. On the other hand, natural stone, particularly granite, has nudged out tile in popularity in recent years. Not only is it rich looking, it is durable. But it is expensive, so you might want to consider a stone look-alike fabricated from solid-surfacing material or another laminate. Another cost-cutting alternative is stone tile, as opposed to slab stone. However, the latter offers more design flexibility.

Hardwood is eye-pleasing, but it will require regular upkeep in a bathroom. Wall-to-wall carpeting and moisture aren't a good marriage either. Consider using washable throw rugs (with non-skid backing) instead to add color, texture, or a pattern on the floor. Resilient-vinyl flooring is a low-cost option that will last at least 20 years and resists mold and mildew.

When you're choosing paint for the walls, look for one that contains mildewcide. Eggshell, satin, or semigloss finishes resist moisture better than a flat paint. Wallpaper is another option. But choose practical moisture-resistant, scrubbable vinyl wallpaper for the best results.

A handsome granite countertop, glass sinks, and floor-to ceiling cabinets create a good-looking bathroom that's designed for two. The large mirror makes the compact space appear larger.

ONE MORE THING...

PROPER VENTILATION should be part of any bathroom design. Bathroom fans usher damaging moisture and odors to the outside. Look for an exhaust fan that can move a lot of air (measured in cubic feet per minute, or *cfm*) without making a lot of noise (measured in sones). Fans can range from 1 sone, which is the quietest model you can buy, to more than 4 sones. Make sure to put the fan on a separate switch so that you don't have to turn it on every time you flick on the light. However, some fans come with a built-in infrared heating unit or a light fixture. Fresh air is always important, too. Combining a fan with an operable window will maximize ventilation.

Access to the outdoors, especially a private deck and hot tub, is the ultimate indulgence.

Fixtures

A trend these days is to compartmentalize various areas in the bathroom. The toilet room, where the fixture is contained in a separate compartment or partially enclosed by a half wall, is an example. While this is great for privacy, it requires space. If you have the room to do it, especially if you will be sharing the bath with two or more people, it makes sense to create individual zones for grooming, toileting, showering, and bathing.

When you shop for a toilet, you'll find two bowl styles: standard and elongated. Two inches longer than the standard models, elongated one-piece toilets are considered more comfortable and sanitary. They fit into contemporary decor, while two-piece models (a separate tank a bowl) come in a range—from Mediterranean to Modern.

With the introduction of the government's WaterSense label (similar to Energy Star), manufacturers are getting smart about reducing toilet water use. Low-flow toilets reduce the amount of water used with each flush. Even more water-efficient, dual-flush toilets, widely used in Europe and Australia, are now available to the U.S. market. If you have an old toilet, upgrade to one of these water-conserving models.

Using ceramic tile and wood creates a spa-like atmosphere, while natural light brightens the room, left. The glass shower keeps the look light.

Sharing a bath isn't all bad, especially if there are separate amenities for each person. Although space is limited in this room, opposite, a pair of modest-size vanities easily accommodate grooming and storage needs for two.

Tubs

A TUB IS MORE THAN JUST A TUB TODAY, but it doesn't have to be sumptuous to be relaxing. A standard 60-inch-long model will do. However, a roomy soaking tub, which usually comes 42 inches wide, certainly has its advantages. Today, you can find a bathtub with a built-in head rest at one end and other convenient options, including drink holders. Or you can look into a vintage or reproduction cast-iron tub with lion's-claw feet. Beyond the typical porcelain, enameled-over cast iron, fiberglass, and acrylic versions, tubs can be made from concrete and mosaic tile, stone, and even wood.

Whirlpool tubs add convenience and comfort while increasing the resale value of your house. They come in all shapes and colors. Some are outfitted with jets that pump water and air at variable speeds. Multiple-jetted tubs can massage your feet or your shoulders. Some high-end extras include colored underwater lights, sound systems, and TV.

Create a private spa. A large tub encased in a stone surround, above, is the perfect escape from daily tension.

Relive the past. A cast-iron tub and black-and-white mosaic tile strike a retro chord in this roomy bathroom, right.

Showers and Lavs

SHOWERS HAVE BECOME the new status symbol in luxury bathrooms. Like whirlpool tubs, showers can now be outfitted with steam, multiple massage jets, or even video and audio equipment. A shower can be designed to be separate from the tub or to take the place of the tub altogether. If you don't like to take a lot of long baths, this makes sense. As with toilets, showerheads now come in water-conserving models, using only 1.6 versus the standard 2.5 gallons per minute.

In small spaces, pedestal lavs are a good choice. Handsome yet compact, they add elegance to a plain bathroom. The only downside? You lose storage space. This may not be a big deal if there is a linen closet in or near the bathroom. Vanity sinks can be surface-mounted or under-mounted, which means the bowl is attached underneath the countertop. An integral sink combines the countertop material and the bowl (typically a solid-surface laminate) in one seamless piece. This makes for easy cleanup. With one sweep of the sponge, the countertop and sink are clean.

Blur the indoor/outdoor line. Rinse off and cool down outside; then step inside for a hot shower after the game, below left.

Bathe in light. A skylight or roof window will brighten a shower with natural light, below.

BATHROOM STORAGE

YOU NEED TO BE CREATIVE about storage, especially in a small bathroom. Keeping the deck of the sink or the vanity top clear of clutter is important. Look for a medicine cabinet with extra-deep shelves that can accommodate rolls of toilet paper, as well as bulky blow dryers and an electric razor. In a small room, build a floor-to-ceiling cabinet in the corner for storage needs. Cabinet manufacturers also make medicine or vanity cabinets that fit snugly in a 90-degree space and shelving units that fit around and above the toilet. You can also install wall shelves or use a three-tiered hanging basket to store soap and hand towels. Baskets can store grooming items, cleaning products, or extra linens, too. Or look behind the bathroom door for bonus space. Install hooks or an over-the-door rack that can hold everything from towels to shampoo.

Tall cabinets make better use of limited space, below.

Open shelving is a serviceable add-on to every bathroom, right.

BATHROOM LIGHTING

Low-voltage spotlights, below, look sleek, but if they are directed straight down, they can cast shadows across the face.

Lighting fixtures above and at the sides of a mirror, opposite top, provide the best illumination for grooming.

Opaque shades add style while diffusing overhead lighting, opposite bottom.

THE DAYS OF A SINGLE CEILING FIXTURE in the bathroom are over. A good lighting plan involves a series of layers—placing ample light where it is needed for bathing or grooming, while other light sources enhance the overall mood of the room.

Vanity lighting is the most important because these fixtures are key to illuminating the head and the face. The most common mistake people make is installing recessed ceiling fixtures directly over the mirror. Recessed lights are fine for general light in a large room, but over a mirror they can cast unflattering shadows on the face, making daily grooming rituals more difficult. Light from above a mirror should be diffused. Better yet, combine it with side fixtures, such as sconces or vertical light bars. If possible, fixtures mounted on either side of a single vanity mirror should be 36 to 40 inches apart. The center of each fixture should be roughly at eye level or about 66 inches above the floor. This will guarantee even illumination across your face.

When sidelights are impractical and you have to use an overhead fixture, install it 75 to 80 inches above the floor. In general, you will need at least 150 watts for grooming.

If the bathroom is small, vanity lights, sconces, or a single ceiling fixture is fine for overall illumination. Fixtures come in all types to match specific architectural and decorative styles and a number of finishes that you can coordinate with the hardware in the room.

Looking for drama? Cove lighting—backlighting a strip of crown molding, for example—can add an even, indirect glow around the perimeter of the room.

A small recessed spotlight can be directed at a piece of art or nice tilework.

Don't forget to light the tub and the shower with fixtures that are intended for moist areas.

ONE MORE THING...

Safety First

ELECTRICITY AND WATER are a dangerous combination and should always be kept as far apart as possible in the bathroom. The National Electrical Code requires all new outlets to have ground-fault circuit interrupters (GFCI); the newer ones can be retrofitted to existing outlets. Even with a GFCI, free-standing plug-in lamps should never be placed near a sink or tub. Fixtures that are going to be within a certain distance of the tub or shower (usually 6 feet, although local codes vary) must be "wet" or "shower-location" rated.

RESOURCES

This list of manufacturers and associations is meant to be a general guide to additional industry and product-related sources. It is not intended as a listing of products and manufacturers represented by the photographs in this book.

All Multimedia Storage

9706 NW Henry Ct.
Portland, OR 97229
866-603-1700
www.allmultimediastorage.com
Manufactures media storage.

Atlantis Cabinetry

3304 Aerial Way Dr.
Roanoke, VA 24018
540-342-0363
www.atlantiscabinetry.com
Manufactures durable, polymer outdoor cabinetry in a variety of colors and designs.

Baldhead Cabinets

20522 Builders St.
Bend, OR 97701
541-749-4260
www.baldheadcabinets.com
Manufactures garage enhancement systems.

Baltic Leisure

601 Lincoln St.
P.O. Box 530
Oxford, PA 19363
800-441-7147
www.balticleisure.com
Manufactures steam showers and saunas.

Barbeques Galore

10 Orchard Rd., Ste. 200
Lake Forest, CA 92630
800-752-3085
www.bbqgalore.com
Retailer of barbecue grills, cooking islands, and accessories.

Benjamin Moore & Co.

51 Chestnut Ridge Rd.
Montvale, NJ 07645
201-573-9600
www.benjaminmoore.com
Manufactures paint for interiors and exteriors.

Bilco

P.O. Box 1203

New Haven, CT 06505

203-934-6363

www.bilco.com

Manufactures window wells and basement doors.

Blue Rhino Corp.

104 Cambridge Plaza Dr.

Winston-Salem, NC 27104

800-762-1142

www.uniflame.com

Offers a full line of grills, heaters, and other outdoor appliances, plus a propane tank exchange program.

Bush Furniture

2081 N. Webb Rd.

Wichita, KS 67206

877-683-9393

www.bush-furniture-online.com

Manufactures home and office furniture.

Cal Spas

1462 9th St.

Pomona, CA 91766

800-225-7727

www.calspas.com

Manufactures barbecue grills, islands, modular islands, fire pits, and fireplaces for the outdoors.

Central Fireplace

20502 106th St.

Greenbush, MN 56726

800-248-4681

www.centralfireplace.com

Manufactures freestanding and zero-clearance fireplaces.

Char-Broil

1442 Belfast Ave.

Columbus, GA 31904

706-571-7000

www.charbroil.com

Manufactures all types of grills, fireplaces, and accessories.

Classic Garden Design

1 Katydid Ln.

Weston, CT

203-226-2886

www.classicgardendesign.com

Designs and installs residential patios, perennial gardens, pergolas, fences, and outdoor kitchens.

Classic Home Elements

540 Gleason Dr.

Moosic, PA 18507

570-774-0057

www.classichomeelements.com

Manufactures outdoor teak and polymer cabinets.

Concrete Encounter

419 Knapps Hwy.

Fairfield, CT 06825

203-659-4765

www.concreteencounter.com

Manufactures concrete countertops, custom sinks, fireplace surrounds, and precast elements.

Consumer Product Safety Commission (CPSC)

4330 East West Hwy.

Bethesda, MD 20814

800-638-2772

www.cpsc.gov

Organization charged with protecting the public from unreasonable risks of serious injury or death from more than 15,000 types of consumer products.

Country Casual

7601 Rickenbacker Dr.

Gaithersburg, MD 20879

800-289-8325

www.countrycasual.com

Designs and manufactures outdoor teak furniture.

Dacor

1440 Bridge Gate Dr.

Diamond Bar, CA 91765

800-793-0093

www.dacor.com

Designs and manufactures a full line of outdoor grills, built-in grills, grill carts, warming ovens, and side burners.

Danver

One Grand St.
Wallingford, CT 06492
888-441-0537
www.danver.com
Produces stainless-steel kitchen cabinets and carts for the outdoors.

DCS by Fisher & Paykel

5900 Skylab Rd.
Huntington Beach, CA 92647
888-936-7872
www.dcsappliances.com
Offers a full line of stainless-steel outdoor grills and grilling systems, including sinks, side burners, and griddles.

Earthstone Wood-Fire Ovens

6717 San Fernando Rd.
Glendale, CA 91201
800-840-4915
www.earthstoneovens.com
Offers reassembled and modular wood- and gas-fired ovens.

Eldorado Stone

31610 NE 40th St.
Carnation, WA 98014
425-883-1991
www.eldoradostone.com
Manufactures veneer stone for outdoor use.

Elfa International AB

888-266-8246
www.elfa.com
Manufactures storage products, including ventilated drawer systems and flexible shelving systems.

Finnleo

575 E. Cokato St.
Cokato, MN 55321
800-346-6536
www.finnleo.com
Manufactures saunas, steam baths, and accessories.

Fire Magic

14724 E. Proctor Ave.
City of Industry, CA 91746
800-332-0240
www.rhpeterson.com
Manufactures infrared grills and other outdoor kitchen products.

Fire Stone Home Products

12400 Portland Ave. S., Ste. 195
Burnsville, MN 55337
866-303-4028
www.firestonehp.com
Offers a full product line for outdoor living, including grills, fireplaces, lighting, and furniture.

Fogazzo Wood Fired Ovens and Barbecues

114 E. St. Joseph Ave.
Arcadia, CA 91006
866-364-2996
www.fogazzo.com
Designs and manufactures wood-fired ovens, barbecues, and fireplaces for the outdoors.

Frigidaire

250 Bobby Jones Expwy.
Martinez, GA 30907
800-374-4432
www.frigidaire.com
Manufactures a full line of outdoor grills, including models with infrared burners.

GarageFloor.com
888-8-Garage
www.garagefloor.com
Manufactures garage-floor products, including tiles, mats, and epoxy.

GarageTek
5 Aerial Way, Ste. 200
Syosset, NY 11791
866-664-2724
www.garagetek.com
Manufactures organization and storage systems for the garage.

GarageWerks
P.O. Box 800
Ada, MI 49301
866-999-3757
www.garagewerks.com
Manufactures flooring and storage solutions for the garage.

Gladiator GarageWorks, a div. of Whirlpool Corp.
2000 M-63 N.
Benton Harbor, MI 49022
866-342-4089
www.gladiatorgw.com
Manufactures garage flooring and storage accessories.

Griot's Garage
3500-A 20th St. E.
Tacoma, WA 98424
800-345-5789
www.griotsgarage.com
Sells everything for the car enthusiast and their garage.

Haier America
1356 Broadway
New York, NY 10018
877-377-3639
www.haieramerica.com
Manufactures major appliances and electronics, such as refrigerators, freezers, and wine coolers.

Hartco Hardwood Floors (div. of Armstrong)
P.O. Box 4009
Oneida, TN 37841
800-769-8528
www.hartcoflooring.com
Manufactures engineered hardwood and solid-wood flooring.

HyLoft USA, LLC
5175 E. Diablo Dr., Ste. 110
Las Vegas, NV 89118
800-990-6003
www.hyloft.com
Manufactures storage products for the home and garage.

Jacuzzi Inc.
14801 Quorum Dr., Ste 550
Dallas, TX 75254
800-288-4002
www.jacuzzi.com
Manufactures spas and shower systems.

JNK Products
1111 S. 7th St.
Grand Junction, CO 81501
877-873-3736
www.jnkproducts.com
Manufactures attic-remodeling supplies, such as pull-down stairs, fans, and flooring, as well as garage products.

Kemiko Concrete Products
P.O. Box 1109
Leonard, TX 75452
903-587-3708
www.kemiko.com
Manufactures acid stains for concrete flooring and other concrete products. Creates decorative concrete floors.

Kohler
444 Highland Dr.
Kohler, WI 53044
800-456-4537
www.kohler.com
Manufactures sinks and faucets.

Kraftmaid Cabinetry, Inc.
P. O. Box 1055
Middlefield, OH 44062
440-632-5333
www.kraftmaid.com
Manufactures cabinetry.

La-Z-Boy, Inc.
1284 N. Telegraph Rd.
Monroe, MI 48162
734-241-4414
www.lazyboy.com
Manufactures furniture including home-theater seating.

Life Fitness
5100 N. River Rd.
Schiller Park, IL 60176
888-348-4543
www.lifefitness.com
Sells home-fitness equipment through a network of specialty fitness retailers and the online store.

Lynx Professional Grills
6023 E. Bandini Blvd.
Commerce, CA 90040
888-879-2322
www.lynxprofessionalgrills.com
Manufactures stainless-steel grills, side burners, refrigerators, warming drawers, and ice machines for the outdoors.

Marvel Industries
P.O. Box 997
Richmond, IN 47375
800-428-6644
www.marvelindustries.com
Manufactures outdoor appliances including refrigerators, ice machines, wine coolers, and beer dispensers.

MultiSport Surfaces, LLC
201-666-4333
www.multisportsurfacesllc.com
Designs and installs court systems and putting greens.

NanaWall Systems, Inc.
707 Redwood Hwy.
Mill Valley, CA 94941
800-873-5673
www.nanawall.com
Manufactures folding-wall systems.

Nautilus
1886 Prarie Wy.
Louisville, CO 80027
800-688-9991
www.nautilus.com
Manufactures exercise equipment, such as the Stairmaster.

Precor USA
P. O. Box 7202
Woodinville, WA 98072
800-786-8404
www.precor.com
Manufactures cardiovascular-fitness equipment, such as elliptical trainers, for residential and commercial use.

Resist-a-ball
4507 Furling Ln., Unit 201
Destin, FL 32541
877-269-9893
www.resistaball.com
Manufactures fitness stability balls and offers exercise workshops and courses for consumers.

Rubbermaid
3320 W. Market St.
Fairlawn, OH 44333
888-895-2110
www.rubbermaid.com
Manufactures home-organization products, such as portable cabinets, storage bins, and toolboxes.

ShadeTree
6317 Busch Blvd.
Columbus, OH 43229
800-894-3801
www.shadetreecanopies.com
Manufactures retractable canopy systems that are water repellant and help block UV rays.

Sherwin-Williams Co.
101 Prospect Ave. N.W.
Cleveland, OH 44115
216-566-2200
www.sherwin-williams.com
Manufactures paint, stain, and wallcovering products.

Sonoma Cast Stone
133A Copeland St.
Petaluma, CA 94952
877-283-2400
www.sonomastone.com
Produces concrete sinks, countertops, and surrounds.

Stanley Furniture
1641 Fairystone Park Hwy.
Stanleytown, VA 24168
276-627-2100
www.stanley.com
Manufactures entertainment centers and other home furniture.

SunBriteTV
5069 Maureen Ln., Unit A
Moorpark, CA 93021
866-357-8688
www.sunbritetv.com
Manufactures all-weather outdoor LCD televisions.

TIC Corp.
15224 E. Stafford St.
City of Industry, CA 91744-4418
626-968-0211
www.ticcorp.com
Designs, produces, distributes, and installs exterior-grade audio systems.

VersaSport
1705 Gulf St.
Lamar, MO 64759
800-540-4899
www.versasport.com
Manufactures court surfaces and flooring systems as well as SofTrak putting greens.

Viking Range Corp.
111 Front St.
Greenwood, MS 38930
662-455-1200
www.vikinrange.com
Manufactures major appliances for indoors and outdoors.

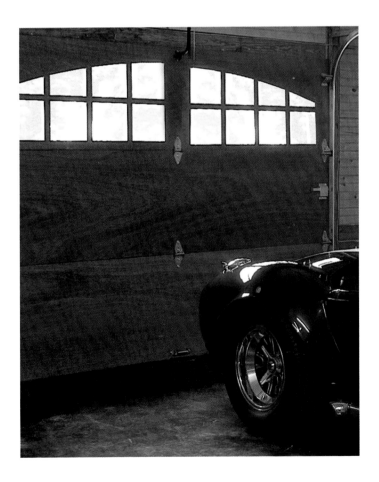

GLOSSARY

Accent lighting Lighting that highlights a space or object to emphasize its character.

Accessible designs Those that accommodate persons with physical disabilities.

Adaptable designs Those that can be easily changed to accommodate a person with disabilities.

Ambient light Also called general light, this overall light fills an entire room.

Armoire A solid cabinet, usually made of wood, that holds entertainment equipment or clothing.

Awning window A single-sash window with a crank that swings outward and is hinged at the top.

Backlighting Illumination coming from a source behind or at the side of an object.

Backsplash The vertical part at the rear and sides of a countertop that protects the adjacent wall.

Bifold door A hinged door, usually on a closet, that folds to the sides when opened.

Built-in Any element, such as a bookcase or cabinet, that is built into a wall or an existing frame.

Bulkhead door A sloping metal door that opens from both sides and covers an exterior stairway into a basement.

Casegoods A piece of furniture used for storage, including cabinets, dressers, and desks.

Casement window A single-sash window with a crank that opens in or out and is hinged on the side.

Casing The exposed trim around windows and doors.

Clearance The amount of space between two fixtures, the centerlines of two fixtures, or a fixture and an obstacle, such as a wall.

Code A locally or nationally enforced mandate regarding structural design, materials, plumbing, or electrical systems that state what you can or cannot do when you build or remodel.

Column A vertical support in a building frame, made of wood, metal, or concrete.

Contemporary Any current design that does not contain traditional or period elements.

Coped joint A curved cut on a piece of trim that makes the reverse image of the piece it must butt against.

Cornice Ornamental trim at the meeting of roof and wall (exterior) or at the top of a wall (interior).

Cove 1. A built-in recess in a wall or ceiling that conceals an indirect light source. 2. A concave recessed molding that is usually found where the wall meets the ceiling or floor.

Dehumidifier A machine that reduces the amount of moisture in the air.

Dimmer switch A switch that can vary the intensity of the light it controls

Double-hung window A window with one or a pair of movable sash that slide vertically within the frame.

Dovetail A joinery method in which wedge-shaped parts are interlocked to form a tight bond. This joint is commonly used in furniture making.

Dowel A short cylinder, made of wood, metal, or plastic, that fits into corresponding holes bored in two pieces of wood, creating a joint.

Drop ceiling A ceiling that is suspended and hides eyesores, such as electrical wires.

Drywall Gypsum sandwiched between treated paper, used as an interior wall covering. Also called gypsum board or wallboard.

Faux finish A decorative paint technique that imitates a texture or pattern found in nature.

Finial   The decorative element on top of a post.

Fittings   The plumbing devices that bring water to the fixtures, such as faucets.

Fluorescent lighting   A glass tube coated on the interior with phosphor, a chemical compound that emits light when activated by ultraviolet energy. Air in the tube is replaced with a combination of argon gas and a small amount of mercury.

Footcandle   A unit that is used to measure brightness. A footcandle is equal to one lumen per square foot of surface.

Framed cabinet   A cabinet with a full frame across the face of the cabinet box.

Frameless cabinet   A cabinet without a face frame. It may also be called a "European-style" cabinet.

French door   A door, typically with 12 divided panes of glass. It can be used alone, in pairs, or as a fixed window.

Frieze   A horizontal band at the top of the wall or just below the cornice.

Full-spectrum light   Light that contains the full range of wavelengths that can be found in daylight, including invisible radiation at the end of each visible spectrum.

Gateleg table   A drop-leaf table supported by a gate-like leg that folds or swings out to support the tabletop.

Glass block   Decorative building blocks made of translucent glass or acrylic for windows or non-load-bearing walls.

Glider   A window with two sash that are set horizontally into a track to slide past each other within one frame. (Also called a slider.)

Ground-fault circuit interrupter (GFCI)   A safety circuit breaker that compares the amount of current entering a receptacle with the amount leaving. If there is a discrepancy of 0.005 volt, the GFCI breaks the circuit in a fraction of a second. GFCIs are required by the National Electrical Code (NEC) in damp areas of the house.

Grout A mortar that is used to fill the spaces between tiles.

Hardware Wood, plastic, or metal-plated trim found on the exterior of furniture or cabinets, such as knobs, handles, and decorative trim.

Harmonious color scheme Also called analogous, a combination focused on neighboring hues on the color wheel. The shared underlying color generally gives such schemes a coherent flow.

Hopper A window that is hinged at the bottom and tilts in when it is open. This is the most common type of basement window.

Impact-resistant glass Interlayers of laminated glass within an exceptionally strong frame that is designed to withstand shattering when stuck by a hard, forceful object or high-speed wind.

Incandescent lighting A bulb (lamp) that converts electric power into light by passing electric current through a filament of tungsten wire.

Indirect lighting A more subdued type of lighting that is not head-on, but rather reflected against another surface, such as a ceiling.

Inlay A decoration, usually consisting of stained wood, metal, or mother-of-pearl, that is set into the surface of an object in a pattern and finished flush.

Joist Horizontal framing lumber placed on edge to support subfloors or hold up ceilings.

Laminated glass Two or three layers of glass with interlayers of plastic or resin, which hold fragments together if the glass shatters.

Louver door A framed door with horizontal slats for admitting air or light.

Lumen The measurement of a source's light output—the quantity of visible light.

Lumens per watt (LPW) The ratio of the amount of light provided to the energy (watts) used to produce the light.

Modular   Units of a standard size, such as parts of a sofa, that can be fitted together.

Molding   An architectural band used to trim a line where materials join or create a linear decoration. It is typically made of wood, plaster, or a polymer.

Murphy bed   A bed that folds into the wall or a closet when not in use.

Opaque shade   A lamp shade that only allows light to escape through the top and bottom.

Partition wall   A non-load-bearing wall built to partition interior space.

Pediment   A triangular element found over doors, windows, and occasionally mantels. It also refers to a low-pitched gable on the front of a building.

Pendant   Fixtures that hang down from the ceiling and direct light upward or downward.

Peninsula   A countertop, with or without a base cabinet, that is connected at one end to a wall or another counter and extends outward, providing access on three sides.

Pocket door   A door that slides into the wall when it is open.

Recessed light   A light that has canister-style housing and is recessed into the ceiling.

Sconce   A decorative wall light that usually focuses light toward the ceiling.

Sectional sofa   A sofa that is comprised of separate pieces that coordinate with each other. The pieces can be arranged together as a large unit or used independently.

Single-hung window   A window with two sash; the bottom one is operable and the top one is stationary.

Slipcover   A fabric cover that can be draped or tailored to fit over a piece of furniture.

Stud   A vertical support element made of wood or metal that is used in the construction of walls.

Tambour door   A cabinet door that is on a track and rolls up or down.

Task lighting   Lighting that focuses on a specific area, such as a computer desk or a work table.

Torchère   A tall floor lamp that resembles a torch and directs light toward the ceiling.

Translucent shade   A lamp shade that diffuses light.

Trompe l'oeil   French for "fools the eye." A style of painting that gives the viewer the illusion of reality.

Uplight   Also used to describe the lights themselves, this is the term for light that is directed upward toward the ceiling.

Veneer   A thin surface layer used on cabinetry and furniture.

Watt   A unit of measurement of electrical power required or consumed by a fixture or appliance.

Window well   A well, sometimes with levels or terraces, that leads to a basement window, allowing natural light to enter into the space.

INDEX

CREDITS

pages 1: Olson Photographic, LLC page 2: Roger Wade page 5: Stan Sudol pages 6–12: *all* Roger Wade page 14: davidduncanlivingston.com page 16: courtesy of Gladiator/Whirlpool page 17: davidduncanlivingston.com pages 18–19: *both* courtesy of Garage Envy Inc. page 20: davidduncanlivingston.com page 22: courtesy of Gladiator/Whirlpool page 23: Olson Photographic, LLC page 24: courtesy of Clopay page 25: davidduncanlivingston.com pages 26–27: *all* courtesy of Gladiator/Whirlpool page 28: Olson Photographic, LLC page 29: *top* courtesy of Gladiator/Whirlpool; *bottom* Olson Photographic, LLC page 30: davidduncanlivingston.com pages 32–33: *all* Olson Photographic, LLC page 34: courtesy of Gladiator/Whirlpool page 35: Tony Giammarino/Giammarino & Dworkin page 36: *top & bottom right* courtesy of Gladiator/Whirlpool; *bottom left* Bradley Olman page 37: courtesy of Clopay pages 38–40: *both* courtesy of Gladiator/Whirlpool page 41: Kenneth Rice pages 42–43: *both* courtesy of Gladiator/Whirlpool page 44: courtesy of Garage Envy Inc. page 45: courtesy of Gladiator/Whirlpool page 46: *left* courtesy of Gladiator/Whirlpool; *right* Kenneth Rice page 47: *top* Olson Photographic, LLC; *bottom* courtesy of Baldhead Cabinets page 48: courtesy of Gladiator/Whirlpool page 49: *top* courtesy of Gladiator/Whirlpool; *bottom* Kenneth Rice page 50: courtesy of Garage Envy Inc. pages 51–54: *all* courtesy of Gladiator/Whirlpool page 55: *top & bottom left* Kenneth Rice; *right* courtesy of Gladiator/Whirlpool page 56: *left* courtesy of

Gladiator/Whirlpool; *right* Stan Sudol page 57: Kenneth Rice page 58: courtesy of Gladiator/Whirlpool page 60: *left* courtesy of Gladiator/Whirlpool; *right* Stan Sudol page 61: Kenneth Rice page 62: Roger Wade page 64: Tria Giovan page 65: *top* davidduncanlivingston.com; *bottom* George Pierce page 66: *left* Eric Roth; *right* Mark Samu pages 67–68: *both* Eric Roth page 69: *top* davidduncanlivingston.com; *bottom* Tria Giovan page 70: davidduncanlivingston.com page 71: *top* davidduncanlivingston.com; *bottom* George Pierce pages 72–73: *all* Roger Wade page 74: *top* Stan Sudol; *bottom* George Pierce page 75: Eric Roth pages 76–77: *both* Roger Wade page 78: *left* Olson Photographic, LLC; *right* George Pierce page 80: *top* George Pierce; *bottom* Olson Photographic, LLC page 81: Eric Roth page 82: *left* George Pierce; *right* Stan Sudol page 83: Roger Wade page 84: *top* Olson Photographic, LLC; *bottom* George Pierce page 85: George Pierce pages 86–96: *all* Stan Sudol page 97: davidduncanlivingston.com page 98: Stan Sudol page 99: Olson Photographic, LLC pages 100–101: *both* Eric Roth page 102: Mark Samu page 103: *top* Garden Collection; *bottom* Eric Roth page 104: Mark Lohman page 105: George Pierce page 106: courtesy of Viking pages 108–110: *both* Roger Wade page 111: courtesy of Viking page 112: courtesy of Nana Wall Systems page 113: courtesy of Viking page 114: courtesy of Shade Tree page 115: Home and Garden Editorial Services page 116: courtesy of Cal Spas page 117: Mark Lohman pages 118–121: *all* courtesy of Viking page 122:

courtesy of Fogazzo Wood Fired Ovens page 123: courtesy of Viking page 124: courtesy of Atlantis Cabinetry pages 125–128: *all* courtesy of Viking page 129: *both* courtesy of Classic Home Elements page 130: courtesy of Viking page 131: courtesy of Classic Home Elements page 132: *top* courtesy of Sunbrite TV; *bottom* courtesy of El Dorado Stone page 133: courtesy of Viking page 134: *top* courtesy of Atlantis Cabinetry; *bottom* courtesy of Danver page 135: *top* courtesy of Viking; *bottom* courtesy of Country Casual page 136: Roger Wade page 138: Donna Chiarelli page 139: Garden Collection page 140: Roger Wade page 141: Stan Sudol page 142: *both* Garden Collection page 143: Andrew Kline/CH page 144: Stan Sudol page 145: *left* Andrew Kline/CH; *right* Eric Roth page 146: Andrew Kline/CH page 147: Garden Collection page 148: Tria Giovan page 149: *top* Garden Collection; *bottom* Stan Sudol page 150: *top* Stan Sudol; *bottom* Tria Giovan page 151: Garden Collection pages 153–165: *all* Eric Roth page 166: davidduncanlivingston.com page 167: Eric Roth page 168: Tria Giovan page 169: davidduncanlivingston.com page 170: Tria Giovan page 171: *top* Eric Roth; *bottom* Roger Wade page 172–173: *all* Eric Roth pages 174–179: *all* Roger Wade page 180: Robin Stubbert pages 181-187: *all* Roger Wade page 188: Jim Westphalen page 190: courtesy of Viking page 191: courtesy of Gladiator/Whirlpool page 193: Olson Photographic, LLC pages 195–199: *all* Roger Wade page 207: Stan Sudol

Have a home improvement, decorating, or gardening project? Look for these and other fine Creative Homeowner books wherever books are sold.

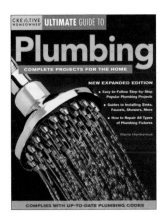

The complete manual for plumbing projects. Over 750 color photos and illustrations. 288 pp.; 8¹/₂" × 10⁷/₈"
BOOK #: 278200

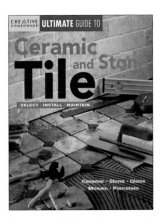

Complete DIY tile instruction. Over 550 color photos and illustrations. 224 pp.; 8¹/₂" × 10⁷/₈"
BOOK #: 277532

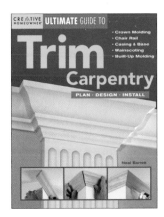

Add trimwork and molding to your home. Over 700 photos and illustrations. 208 pp.; 8¹/₂" × 10⁷/₈"
BOOK #: 277516

The ultimate home-improvement reference manual. Over 300 step-by-step projects. 608 pp.; 9" × 10⁷/₈"
BOOK #: 267870

A complete guide, covering all aspects of drywall. Over 450 color photos. 160 pp.; 8¹/₂" × 10⁷/₈"
BOOK #: 278320

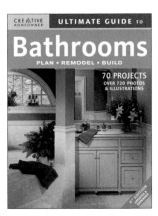

Includes step-by-step projects and over 580 photos. 272 pp.; 8¹/₂" × 10⁷/₈"
BOOK #: 278632

Transform a room with trimwork. Over 550 color photos and illustrations. 240 pp.; 8¹/₂" × 10⁷/₈"
BOOK #: 277500

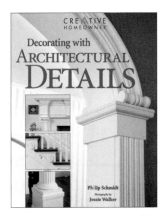

Covers design treatments such as moldings and window seats. 300+ color photos. 224 pp.; 8¹/₂" × 10⁷/₈"
BOOK #: 278225

Newly revised, with all the answers for a new kitchen. Over 500 color photographs. 224 pp.; 8¹/₂" × 10⁷/₈"
BOOK #: 279415

Newly revised, with all you need to know to design a bath. Over 500 color photos. 224 pp.; 8¹/₂" × 10⁷/₈"
BOOK #: 279268

An impressive guide to garden design and plant selection. 950 color photos and illustrations. 384 pp.; 9" × 10"
BOOK #: 274610

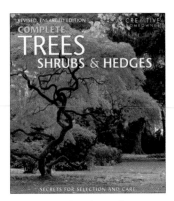

How to select and care for landscaping plants. More than 700 photos. 240 pp.; 9" × 10"
BOOK #: 274222

For more information and to order direct, visit our Web site at **www.creativehomeowner.com**